DROPS OF LIFE EXPERIENCE

BY

CHANTAL AGAPITI

Copyright © 2023 Chantal Agapiti
All rights reserved.

Contents

DROP ONE: A MICRO MEMOIR	7
1.1 D-DAY	9
1.2 FROZEN	14
1.3 WRITING	21
1.4 MY DISABILITY	28
DROP TWO: STORIES OF LIFE	33
2.1 LOVE	35
2.2 GROWTH	47
2.3 WORK	77
2.4 PARENTHOOD	100
2.5 CHANGE	108
DROP THREE: POEMS OF LIFE	125
DROP FOUR: THOUGHTS ON LIFE	177
CONCLUSION	232

"'If you can't help everyone, just help one.'

This is the spirit on which I created

the Facebook page *Drops of Life Experience*,

helping others, motivating, and, hopefully, helping each other.

This is my personal space in which I can express myself freely.

Discussing topics related to my personal experience.

That's what makes this different, as I'm not a professional;

however, I have something that can't be taught, 'life' experience.

I'm highly sensitive and empathetic, and I care.

Let's make every 'drop' count."

This was the first post I published on LinkedIn in 2016.

Acknowledgments

This book is dedicated to my kids, Dante and Gianluca.
You are my light in the darkness.
I loved you even before you were on your way to this world and you truly became mine, in essence.

A special thank you to my husband for sticking with me through my struggles. Thanks for believing in my capabilities to become the writer I always was, but didn't have the courage to be.

A special mention to some amazing souls: Rachael Lemon and Isabel Gomez. I hope you both know what you mean to me. You're proof there are still genuine people in this world. Always there for me, expecting nothing in return but friendship.

And last but not least, a big thank you to my online community for your support and precious insights. You are an inspiration to me.

To my inner child, I say

Thank you for holding on, for not giving up.

Something good has come of it.

This is my hug to you.

Introduction

My Imagination Has Been a Life Savior.

I've been to hell and back, yet I'm still here to tell my story.

My life has been more vivid than a movie, more telling than a book, and more imaginative than a story. I've lived through some of the worst things that can happen to a person, to a woman in particular. Murphy's Law had his sadistic way with me. Trauma, lies, and deception have been a certainty for a significant part of my life. Solitude was a loyal companion, but my imagination has been an absolute life savior, and my strong will a trusted copilot.

The only good that came out of it was that I didn't allow it to crush me, even if it was a close call. Over time, I gained strength and perseverance instead. I never had anything the easy way, and I had to keep my head down and do the work to make things happen in my life. I received no help or support throughout my childhood; maybe I had to grow up too soon, but I *did* grow up too soon. Therefore, I made mistakes along the way, trusted the wrong people, and fell in love with narcissists. But that could happen to anybody, as narcissists don't have a tattoo on their forehead stating, "Just get away while you still can. Get up and run!"

When you haven´t received love as a child, you don't know what it is or what to look for. And I was in desperate need of love throughout a big part of life, especially before my accident, which would change everything. The first time I fell in love was in kindergarten. I'm just saying I didn't have a healthy approach toward it and didn't know how to recognize it, even if my life depended on it. If a boy was nice to me, gave me attention, or just noticed I was standing there, well, that was good enough for me. Add some bad-boy looks and attitude, and I was hooked.

Every time things went sour, I felt hurt, as if I were going to die that instant, and I cried my eyes out and kept asking myself, *Why is this happening to me? Why are you doing this to me?* And the ugly truth to these questions came only after my car accident fourteen years ago. I suffered from insomnia for months afterward and spent hours looking at my life, searching for answers. Since I had survived, I believed my accident had to be a wake-up call, so there must have been a reason for this second chance at life.

One night, it hit me.

One night it hit me; those things happened to me because I let them happen; they hurt me because I let them do it. I can only say that this insight hurt like hell, knowing I had done this to myself. There was no victim here. I had been trying to destroy myself; I was sabotaging my own life. But why would anyone do this to themselves? Because someone made me believe that's what I deserved; someone made me think I wasn't worthy of anything good; someone made me believe I was useless.

And when that someone is the same person who put you on this earth, the one person you should be able to trust blindfolded, the one person who should always have your best interests at heart, well, in the end, you believe it too if it weren't for my accident when the universe made me look at my life and search for answers, who knows if I might have succeeded in ruining my life altogether. Life gave me a second chance, and as soon as my eyes opened that night, I grabbed this gift with both hands.

But this wasn't that kind of gift, beautifully wrapped in paper with a ribbon around it. No, this was a gift covered in thorns, as I had to prove that I had learned my lesson—or so it felt. I had to prove I would stop living in survival mode like I had been doing until then. I would learn to respect myself and make others respect me too. I would trust fate to show me the path to love and how to stop seeking it in the lap of guys who didn't know how to love.

Achieving the knowledge I needed to move on would cost me blood, sweat, and tears. Even if life has a cynical way of making you see things when you least expect it, irony has always found a way to become an uninvited guest. As I was waiting for signs, it seemed I already knew what I needed to do all along. But for some reason, I didn't do it.

Life can be frustrating like that, but it can be pretty rewarding too. I found a quote from Alfred Einstein online that said, "*There are only two ways to live your life. One is as though nothing is a miracle. The other is as though everything is a miracle.*" And that's a beautiful way of expressing a notion that every one of us should be taught from a young age. It should be taught in elementary school, for that matter. Our mind is capable of many things, and it is such a powerful tool. Our motherboard doesn't just save memories; it's also capable of editing how we see life as a whole.

As I always say, it's all about mindset; you've got the power to change things.

Yes, our mind can decide how we perceive and feel about things that happen to or around us. We can manage our view of the world, and we can choose to feel happy or lousy about it. Our mind is such a beautiful tool, but we use it far too little. Maybe because we aren't aware of it or nobody taught us how to use it. That's why I feel this is so important, and I share this knowledge with whomever I can, first of all, with you.

Even though I've suffered a great deal in my life, and despite all the trauma I went through, I'm still capable of love and empathy, as I have always believed something good must come from it all. I couldn't bear the thought that the challenges we endure are just random events. Finding meaning is vital to being apt to move forward and heal. And sharing is the first step toward healing.

Mental health has become a hot topic worldwide. It's not so marginalized anymore, yet the concept of seeking help still hasn't been accepted by all. Society assumes that mental health issues exist and acknowledges the struggles some of us undergo; but when it comes to seeing a therapist, a dark cloud still surrounds the notion. As if going to a therapist means there's something wrong or dangerous about you or that the struggle you're dealing with is of a different caliber. But that's such a misconception. When there is an underlying pathology, you'll be treated by a psychiatrist (who is a physician), and they can prescribe medication to help you manage your illness.

A therapist is not the same thing, and anyone can use Google to find a therapist and book an appointment. You're not sent to see a therapist by your general practitioner, and you're free to assess for yourself if you need to talk to a therapist. This is a healthy and courageous move, as admitting to yourself that you need help and going out and searching for it is a synonym for strength and courage. Bravo to you!

It's like talking to a close friend who keeps it to himself.

For those still in doubt, try to see it as speaking to an outsider to get another's perspective on your troubles. It's like talking to a close friend, but a friend with the needed background and experience to understand what you're dealing with and who can help you see things from a different angle. Someone who gives you an objective way to look at your struggles, and who guarantees your issues won't leave the room. Whatever you say will stay between you and your therapist.

I think it's a safe assumption that we can't get that same kind of guarantee from some of our friends, right? And when we find ourselves stuck in a mind loop, overthinking, we tend to fess up to someone we wouldn't have originally chosen. That's a risk you take when holding everything in for a long time. So please, don't wait for it to grow out of proportion and seek help before it gets too heavy for you to carry.

I wrote this book to help, support, and motivate fellow trauma survivors and chronic pain/illness warriors like me. By sharing my life's stories and the lessons I've learned along my path, I wish to make you see that there are ways to improve your quality of life, despite your inner struggle. Life is too short; for all we know, this is the main event, no rerun, so we owe it to ourselves to make the best of it. As Jack Dawson (Leonardo DiCaprio) said in Titanic, "To make every day count." And we can do that.

Some of you may already know me from social media, where I have been writing consistently for some time now. But my purpose is to reach a larger audience, as the ones who need to hear my message might not be on one of those platforms. I joined them to enhance my purpose, reach more people, and spread my drops of life experience. If I can positively touch one person's life, well, that would be a dream come true.

Let's make every drop count.

I've put my best writing in this book, but I understand that not everyone enjoys reading poetry or that they might like to jump from topic to topic. You decide how you read this book from now on. But I would suggest trying it all, as everything deserves a chance to be read. I share my life's stories in different forms or drops. Why do I call it drops? As Mother Teresa said, "We know only too well that what we are doing is nothing more than a drop in the ocean. But if the drop were not there, the ocean would be less because of that missing drop."

Let's make every drop count.

DROP ONE:

A MICRO MEMOIR

This micro memoir tells

some specific events from my life

that are vital for you to read.

They are essential drops for

You to understand

the "why"

of my purpose.

1.1 D-Day

I put my hand in front of me just as the car in front was about to hit us (or maybe we were just about to hit them), and then I felt my body shifting to the left. The car took us to the opposite side of the road and quickly headed toward the concrete wall that divided the lanes on the highway. As our car was about to crash into that gray wall, I remember thinking this would hurt; hitting that wall would hurt.

But I didn't want to hit that wall; I badly wanted to escape this situation, yet I couldn't, so I closed my eyes and managed to shut off my mind. And it almost worked, as I don't remember hitting the wall, and I have no recollection of the impact. But I did feel the tumbling. The sensation felt like I was lying inside a wooden crate, rolling down a hill. Just as when we were kids, and we rolled ourselves down a hill, we would keep doing it time and time again. It was fun, right?

Wrong. This time, I wasn't having fun at all. This time, I only wanted it to stop; the rolling feeling needed to stop because I couldn't take it anymore. But it kept going, and I was screaming in my head, telling it to stop since I couldn't bear another roll. Yet we kept rolling until it did stop, and the car came to a halt.

Then there was complete silence.

I believe I lost consciousness at that point, as I don't remember immediately waking up. I remember trying to open my eyes, but I couldn't. Just like when you are sound asleep in the morning and your eyes protest, not wanting to open; well, it felt exactly like that. Still, I kept trying until I began to see something, yet my vision was blurry (one of my contacts had fallen out, so I could only see out of one eye). I looked around, but I couldn't make sense of what happened or where I was. I understood I was still in the car, but something was off. After hitting the concrete wall, the vehicle rolled three times to its left, so I was hanging in the air, held up by my seatbelt.

My seatbelt saved my life. All the things that were inside the vehicle were later found on the road. Even my sneakers came off my feet and flew out of the car. So, it doesn't take a genius to understand what would have happened to me if I hadn't put on my seatbelt. Cynically, the very seatbelt that saved my life was the one that crushed me into pieces. The seatbelt was so tight it crushed my thorax, making it almost impossible for me to take in any air. I really needed to breathe some fresh air.

That's when I heard the driver in the seat next to me asking me if I was all right. Sure, dummy, I'm super-duper. I was thinking a variety of bad things at the time, but I kept them to myself. Oh boy, did I have other things on my mind. I asked him to help me, as I couldn't breathe. Even talking required a lot of effort, and it hurt like hell. He pushed on the release button, and my seatbelt came loose. I instantly fell out of the sky (that's how it felt) and landed on my knees. Little did I know that both my legs were broken, as until that point, I didn't feel a thing other than the crushing pain I felt in my chest.

But now that I had some relief from it, I could also feel the other aches. I was holding my body weight on my broken legs, and it felt like my head was about to explode from the pain. There are no words to describe it. I noticed people surrounding the car, trying to get a look inside the vehicle, and I screamed to get me out of there, as I couldn't bear staying in that position. "Just get me out of here!" I yelled. But nobody moved; they just kept staring into the car, talking to each other.

Talk about luck.

Speaking of luck, the car we were in was an old 4x4 with a removable textile top. So, I kept yelling. I don't know for how long, but it felt like forever. Then I heard voices coming closer, asking me to calm down, as help was on its way, but I needed help now, not later. I needed someone to help at that moment. Then a man at the scene said he would get me out. He started unbuttoning the textile cover and removing it from the car; I could see the sunlight shining for the first time since the crash. He grabbed me under my armpits, yanked me out of there, and laid me on the asphalt, which felt like a sauna bench.

It was August, and it had been a sunny day, so the asphalt was quite warm. The warmth from the road was soothing as I lay there waiting; all I could do was look at the sky. I don't remember anything else, only staring at the blue sky, searching for clouds. It felt like I was dosing off since I was tired from the pain, using up all my energy. I didn't think. I just laid there and stared.

Could I hear the sirens? I thought so, but they sounded so far away. The accident happened right when traffic was getting dense from everyone driving home from work. So, even the ambulance was stuck in traffic (irony, my uninvited guest). I could hear the sirens just fine, but they seemed to be lost somewhere nearby. Yet, all the way out there. By then, I had no sense of time, so I can't say how long it took for the ambulance to reach us. I only remember feeling relieved when it did, and from the moment the paramedics approached me, it all proceeded quickly. I used to be a nursing auxiliary, so I could appreciate their professionalism and efficacy, being the one in need this time.

It was only then that I realized what clothes I was wearing, the first time I had a moment of "casual human" thought since the crash. To lower the risk of other injuries, they put me in a vacuum mattress, but they needed to cut my clothes to put me in it. Me, "the prude," being undressed by some strangers in front of a crowd in the middle of the highway . . . It was a scene right out of a teenage nightmare, yet this whole event was an actual nightmare.

At that moment, though, I didn't make a sound, didn't struggle, and just let them do their job. The only thing that went through my mind was how I hated having my favorite jeans and leather jacket cut to shreds. I was still a woman, after all, with human feelings.

I felt like a pearl, comfy in its oyster shell.

They removed the air from the mattress in no time, and it held me snug and safe, like a refuge. I felt as if I were a pearl, comfy in its oyster shell. The paramedics put me on the stretcher and into the back of the ambulance. I saw one of the men standing there, holding the perfusion with the morphine I so needed. However, he had to wait for the emergency doctor to arrive and give him the green light. Again, I was lying down, staring above me; but this time, I was looking at the white metal ambulance ceiling, waiting for the emergency doctor to arrive.

Drops of Life Experience

Once again, I could hear the sirens, yet they seemed lost somewhere in the distance, not getting any closer. Even the paramedic was losing his patience. In the meantime, he followed protocol and kept me awake and alert by asking my name and age . . . over and over again. But it hurt to talk. It hurt to even get a gasp of air in my lungs. So, I got mad and asked him to please shut up and stop asking me these stupid questions, as he already knew the answer to them by now.

He smiled and said he was glad to see I was still there. The other ambulance came, and the emergency doctor made a quick assessment and gave the green light to give me morphine, which I welcomed with open arms.

I just wanted to close my eyes and rest for a while, but the paramedic wouldn't let me. Like a watchdog, he would bark whenever I dosed off a little. I heard the double doors closing at my feet and the ambulance moving, but I didn't know where it would take me. One thing was for sure; it would take me to uncharted territory.

1.2 Frozen

The aftermath.

The first month after the accident was the hardest, as I was utterly bedbound, meaning I depended completely on the help of others. I hadn't met my husband yet, so I was still single and lived with my best friend, Dino. He was a stray dog that I had taken in, and he soon became the best friend I had ever had. If it weren't for his love and affection, I wouldn't have made it through—that's for sure.

In the beginning, the only way I had to get out of bed was with a wheelchair, but due to the pain in my lower back, I couldn't stay in it for more than fifteen minutes. After the wheelchair came the crutches, which I had to use for about six months, then I needed just one; and then in March of 2010, I finally didn't need any support at all. I could walk by myself again; what a relief.

During those months, I underwent physical rehabilitation every day. I managed to get back to work in December of that year, part-time at first and then full-time six months later. The same surgeon who operated on me the evening of the crash, removed the titanium insert from my right Tibia about a year later. The bone was healed. Things were looking good for me, and it seemed as if I was getting my life back in order. It almost resembled my life up to the day of my accident.

Fast-forward to 2015, when I was still working full-time; but then August came, and for the first time, I sensed something was off. I always enjoyed working; it gave me a sense of belonging, and I was good at it. Yet that summer morning, I remember getting out of the house, closing the door behind me, still holding the key in the door, and as I looked at my car parked in the driveway, I was frozen on the spot.

This had never happened to me before. I just stood there holding my key in the keyhole, staring at my car. I heard a voice in my head saying, What are you doing? Why are you standing there? Just go, or you'll be late for work. But I couldn't get my body to move. I don't know how many minutes I stood there, but it was quite a few. This was the first clear sign my body gave me, telling me something was wrong. But I had no idea why this happened or what it meant.

I called in sick and experienced severe headaches for the next two weeks. My physiotherapist said the headaches came from tension in my neck and were often caused by stress. Stress? That wasn't anything new to me. I've had anxiety for years, but this had never happened before. I still couldn't see the bigger picture. At that time, burnout was yet to become a renowned term. There were some cases, but most doctors still considered them isolated events. They didn't connect the dots, and neither did I.

It's not a mainstream phenomenon.

So, I proceeded like anyone would; as soon as my headaches improved, I returned to work as if nothing had happened. I didn't even think about that summer morning's episode anymore. I worked just as I always did for another couple of months until June 2016. The project I was working on ended, and after a time, I found myself at home with nothing to do. Summer wasn't a great time to find a new job, so I stayed home caring for my two kids.

But then all hell broke loose. My best friend, Dino, who had kept me together after my accident, was diagnosed with cancer. I still remember crying like a baby, and I couldn't stop. I felt as if my heart was shattered into pieces. The heartaches I experienced when I believed I was in love didn't compare. No, this was a different kind of heartache, the mother of all sorrows that leaves you scarred for life. The kind that changes you forever; the kind that makes you lose an essential part of who you are.

He died in October of that year,
and a part of me died with him that night.

That was the first time I could tell I had become depressed. I know many of us use that term whenever we have a terrible day, but no, I mean it to the full extent of its meaning. It wasn't just grief; I was feeling a void within, as if a part of me had been removed and nothing mattered. I did my best to do what was expected; I cared for my kids and helped around the house. That was all my autopilot was capable of doing. I spent most of the time alone in my bedroom. I just wanted to be left alone in my dark place, feeling empty and miserable.

As days, weeks, and months passed, my dark state shifted from closing myself off to overthinking. My mind was filled with reflections about my life, work, and kids. In other words, I was worrying about everything. My husband and I couldn't have been further apart, and we weren't in sync as we lived in different realities and stages of life. I couldn't relate to him, and he couldn't relate to me. At some point, he said, "You were the strongest woman I had ever met. Now I don't even recognize you anymore." Ouch, an uppercut right to the jaw . . .

So, I joined a group on social media, a private group for people with burnout. I still wasn't sure that was what was happening to me, yet I could relate to what members were posting, and it gave me some sense of belonging and understanding. I tried to share some of my insights with my husband, but he wasn't up for it. He didn't believe I was in the same state as those members; and he even expressed concern about me reading their comments, as they could influence me in some way.

A sense of rare lucidity struck.

I didn't share his concern, as I still felt I was the same intelligent person I had been before. And I wouldn't let myself be influenced by things I didn't believe to be valid. I still had a brain and intended to use it. I remember reading a woman's post, stating that her husband was insensitive and didn't care for her because he didn't ask her anything when he came home from work. She felt ignored and unloved. When I read that, a sense of rare lucidity struck as I thought, *Wait a minute, that man doesn't have a crystal ball. How would he even know if she isn't sharing her feelings with him?*

At that moment, I realized I was doing the same thing in my marriage. I neglected one of the essential parts of any relationship: communication. My husband and I were in different stages of our lives, but that didn't mean we should stop sharing and communicating altogether. And that's what happened, and I let it happen. It's easy to blame someone, but we should also put ourselves in their shoes. Our partners "lost" their trusted partner and didn't understand what was happening. They, too, have thoughts and feelings and worry about it. They, too, deserve to be listened to.

That evening, as soon as my husband came home from work, I went straight to the door and hugged him. I owned up to my part and apologized, and he apologized too. We both felt lighter and understood each other for the first time in months. From that moment on, I would do my best to communicate more, and he would too. Even if we didn't see eye to eye about everything, at least we were sharing, which might have saved our marriage from drowning.

I was in too deep to get myself out.

Still, I knew something deeper was happening inside me, something I couldn't solve alone. I knew talking about it with my husband wouldn't help either since he couldn't relate, no matter how much he tried to. So, I decided to go to a therapist, as I needed an outside and objective view. I was in too deep to get myself out alone.

The therapist listened to me; she let me talk about whatever I wanted to and asked me some questions from time to time. The sessions went fine, but I wasn't making the progress I needed to feel like myself again. I didn't know who I was anymore, since I hadn't felt like myself since Dino's passing. Stuck in a loop, overthinking everything for so long that I wasn't sure about much anymore. I, the independent woman who learned everything by herself, had no clue. Ironic, right?

After weeks of sessions, I just went and asked my therapist what she thought I was going through, as I wasn't sure it was burnout. Yet, burnouts come in different sizes and shapes, so not all experiences are the same. Then she added, "I believe your main issue is an existential crisis. You lost yourself, and you don't recognize the life you live in. You should make some core changes to discover who you are now and who you want to be tomorrow."

DROPS OF LIFE EXPERIENCE

It was my body trying to make me see.

She was correct; I knew it as soon as I heard it. But I still didn't know what significant changes I needed to make in my life. Then I remembered the day I just stood there with my key in the keyhole, staring at my car in the driveway, frozen on the spot. I remembered that moment for the first time in almost two years, and for once, I recognized it as the first clear sign my body gave me. My body tried to make me see and realize something, yet I didn't get it then. But I do now.

Where was I about to go that morning? To work. But why would my body withhold me from going to work in such a way? I'd always liked working, or did I?

When I didn't graduate from nursing school, I was so mad that I took off to follow my lifelong dream: to move to Italy. I didn't expect to flunk, and it felt so unfair, as my grades were good and always had been. I had started nursing school because I wanted to help others, which made me happy. But when I received the bad news, I went to Italy and looked for a job. Any job.

I found one thanks to my linguistic abilities; I'm fluent in four languages and found a job in customer service. Oh, I was so happy because I could stay in Italy to live my dream, and I felt proud because I didn't let adversity get in the way. That's how I began my career, which would last for a decade, until 2016. No passion there, no dream, no real purpose. I just went with what life gave me at the time, and I never thought of doing anything else since I was good at it. And the pay was good too. I just went with the flow and never looked back until that day.

Chantal Agapiti

It told me to stop.

So, that summer morning in 2015, it wasn't a coincidence that my body made me freeze on the spot, withholding me from going to the office. It told me to stop going to *that* work, as I was fed up with it, but I didn't realize it until then. And I began remembering other episodes, too, other little red flags throughout the years that I didn't understand. I had many "aha" moments. (Oh yes, irony strikes again.)

I understood I had to make some significant changes, and I could see I needed to start by changing the kind of work I had been doing for the past ten years. It was easier said than done, as it was a career I was invested in, and now I would have to start all over again. To do what? I thought about what parts of my job as a customer service representative I liked. Why did I enjoy it? I enjoyed it because of the help I gave my customers; it made me feel useful. Another "aha" moment was the link between being an auxiliary nurse and a customer service rep. I was able to help others. That has been my core talent all along.

1.3 Writing

Now I knew what I had to look for in a job to be happy; all I had to do was take all the pieces of the puzzle and assemble them. I can't believe it took me forty-one years to realize that what I liked to do as a child was the one thing I was supposed to be doing in my adult life: writing. My imagination has been a true lifesaver throughout my life, especially during my childhood, as it was the only escape I had found from my so-called home.

I started writing in elementary school; I must have been eight or maybe nine years old. My first work was a novel, a fantasy tale about a young girl who seemed like everyone else, yet she was a goddess with special powers. I called her Olivia, like one of my dolls. Olivia had to reveal her true identity and leave for an adventure to face a demon and save the earth. It's easy to understand that I was writing about myself and dreaming about having the strength to fight back, which I didn't have as a young child, facing the darkness in my own home.

Still, it was a good thing to find solace in writing, and it was my only way to evade and go on imaginary adventures. Through my writing, I was dreaming about being free to explore the world—until I would be old enough to do it for real. When I went to secondary school, I started writing in a journal; and writing became a way to express myself, not through a fantasy story trying to escape my life, but by writing about what I went through in my everyday life and reflecting on it. Through writing, I could examine my issues and find a way out.

I always believed this couldn't be it.

Thinking of myself as a child gives me chills, as I'm still amazed by how that little girl managed to cope with it all; a strong will helped me push on, and the will to live and the hope for something better ahead of me kept me going. I always believed this wasn't it; it couldn't be, because what would even be the point? I was a natural-born critical thinker; and if something didn't make sense (which happens more than you would expect), I would try and dissect it until I found a plausible explanation.

And that process was going on inside my head or on paper through writing, as I had no voice at all. I mastered the art of making people forget I was even there. I thought that would limit the chances of getting hit or cursed at. If only I could make myself small, silent, and insignificant, maybe she would forget about me. But it didn't work, no matter how hard I tried. The thing is, neither I nor my behavior triggered the abuse; her frustration started the abuse. Writing was my way of coping. Hers was something else, or should I say someone else . . .

When I reached the young age of thirty-five, my career counseling coach made me realize I was an introverted, highly sensitive person. Wow, another "aha" moment, as I had always felt different from everyone else, and now I knew why. Because I am different at a neurological level, I have lived without a filter. All that happened around me came right through, at full speed, none diluted. That explains so much. I didn't enjoy loud places, a lot of people crowded in one spot, bright lights, etc. It all got me wired up and increased my stress level.

Drops of Life Experience

I had never heard about HSP.

At that time, I had never heard of the term highly sensitive person, but I Googled it as soon as I got home, and I found many articles and videos explaining it. I used one of those to show my husband that being highly sensitive impairs me in every aspect of my life. I avoid many activities because I know what to expect. It's yet another invisible ache that no one understands, and people think I'm antisocial. But I'm not; I'm not myself because of all the clutter making its way inside me without a filter.

Have you ever been in a public space or in the privacy of your home and suddenly felt like there were too many people in the room? As if the noise of people talking or the music playing is getting louder and louder? Being an introverted, highly sensitive person, I often find myself in this kind of situation, which is completely normal to most. However, I'm looking for a way out.

If you can relate, walk away and get some physical distance whenever it gets too much to handle. Go outside for a breath of fresh air, or go to another room and gather yourself for as long as you need. Grant yourself some time out. In many sports, the coach can ask for a time out to gather his team and motivate his players, so why shouldn't you apply the same tactic in your life?

So be a good coach to yourself and take a time out whenever you need it.

Thanks to Google, you can explain it to others once you have a name for it and you have social proof. Still, it seemed they weren't impressed or convinced. As with all invisible things, only those who can relate to it will understand you. The ones who don't will continue to believe whatever they want, and whatever they feel is the truth, no matter what you tell them. How convenient, right?

Despite all the "aha" moments, it still took me another six years to embrace my purpose and go ahead with my mission to help others through writing. But it doesn't matter how long it took, as I was silent for too long; but now that I have found my voice, I will make sure it gets heard. I'll do all I can to increase my reach to get to those who need to listen to it, people like you and me. That's how this book was born, as I'm living proof that sometimes you need to listen to the right words to realize what you have to do.

I'm one of you.

Superpowers? I have none and I'm not a physician. I'm one of you. A woman, a wife, a mother, a neurodivergent, a trauma survivor, and a chronic pain warrior. That's what I have to offer you, my life experience and the lessons I've learned along the way. It's a process, as it could take years to recover from trauma, and you need to embrace the time it will take and have only one goal at heart: getting better. I emphasize the word "better," as that's what I'm talking about in terms of changing your mindset and enabling you to improve your quality of life.

The first step toward healing is sharing. If you're not ready to talk about it, try to write about it in a journal. Nobody has to see it; nobody even has to know about it. As long as you're sharing your inner struggles on the white pages, that will be the first step toward healing. And as long as you're moving forward, it will still be progress, no matter how slow the process is. Every step you take will bring you that much closer to your goal of getting better.

I'm here to help, support, and motivate you through my words. From this moment on, it's all up to you. You decide how you'll share, choose how long it will take, and decide every step you take. As long as you don't stand still, as long as you keep moving, you'll be one step closer; you'll be one percent better than you were the day before. It's as simple as that; there is no need to complicate it or start overthinking. And if you do, stop and take a deep breath for as long as you need to. Breathing brings you a step closer to where you want to be.

You can share from your safe place.

If you have questions or any doubts or wish to share some thoughts with me, don't hesitate to contact me through social media. That's the beauty of the age we live in; we can get in touch with each other even though we won't ever meet. You can share from your safe place, and I can do the same.

It's important to embrace the change you'll go through, though it might be challenging at times. Sharing your deepest feelings, even on paper, can be pretty uncomfortable at first. You may want to cry at times; that's your body's way of liberating itself from things that are weighing you down. We're often so far gone in our automatic pilot or survival mode that admitting to yourself what you're feeling inside can be quite emotional and even painful.

That's all part of the process, and it's normal to feel different things and have your body react to them. That only proves you're human, and it would be odd if you didn't feel a certain way about it. It's a body and mind voyage; no part is left out, as the journey affects both sides. You'll feel lighter in your head and your body. Because by sharing, you're letting go of the burden within you. Once you share, you're tossing out all the clutter in your mind, which will benefit your body too.

Master the fine art of letting go.

It took me years to master the fine art of letting go, and it was one of the hardest things I ever had to learn. I was quite a pro at overthinking, dissecting every event, and sometimes crying myself to sleep. I felt everything so deeply that my emotions took over, affecting my entire being. If you can relate, let me give you a piece of advice; if you recognize this type of behavior, please stop and learn how to let it go. The sooner, the better, as it's not worth the harm you cause yourself and your loved ones. Start sharing today, this instant, whether through writing or by talking to someone; don't wait any longer. This is your moment; grasp it with both hands.

Drops of Life Experience

THIS IS YOUR PERSONAL SPACE

Your journal

FEEL FREE TO WRITE WHATEVER YOU WANT

1.4 My Disability

My body never returned to its former state.

Since my car accident in '09, my life has made a 180-degree turn. I didn't recognize myself anymore. After years of undergoing physical rehabilitation, going back to work full-time, and having my kids, my body took quite a hit. It never returned to its former state. On the contrary, as time passed and life went on, my body presented me with the bill. But it didn't matter how I felt or where it hurt; the days lasted twenty-four hours; the moon shined at night, and the sun rose in the east and set in the west. I had to keep going and try to keep up with life.

In 2010, I met my husband and married him a year and a half later. Just a short time later, we built a home and had two wonderful gifts: our boys. They are only thirteen months apart, so they behave like twins. Both pregnancies caused some additional strain on my already injured body, as they were both risky. How could it be otherwise, right? I've never gotten the easy path, not even with my pregnancies.

So, with time, the physical aches and the consequences got worse. I went from working full-time to part-time to hybrid. Yet the situation only went downhill. No matter what I did, my body was just worn out. I had no energy and no strength, no bright side whatsoever.

I felt useless to myself, to my family, and to society.

As of September 2021, I was 100 percent unemployed. So, I had another problem to go through and another kind of stress adding up. I was alone in the company of my forever pain, trapped in my aching body, and stuck in an empty house. Day in, day out. Every single day of my life.

Despite the dark state of my mind, which is inevitable when you're going through an invisible battle, all by yourself, my mind was still present. I was still there underneath all that clutter and had plans and dreams to realize. So, I decided to fight back and take matters into my own hands. I would do everything I could to get better and improve my quality of life, even if just a little bit.

And every drop counts, remember? I still believed there was more to this life than pain and struggle. Therefore, I took the initiative and scheduled some medical consultations, saw doctors and specialists, and underwent a lot of tests. All this took quite some time, so I had to be patient and have faith. I had no energy to do anything more at that time. I was waiting and hoping, hoping and waiting. After almost a year, the verdict finally came in the spring of 2022:

Chronic widespread pain, better known as fibromyalgia.

The bad news was that there was no cure. The good news was that I finally knew what was happening to me. It wasn't all in my head, as some dared to say. Knowing what was happening with my body allowed me to have some closure, another "aha" moment that made me realize other things too. I knew what I was battling against, so I could revise a game plan to improve, cope, make the best of it, and make it count.

Society seemed not to be interested in me anymore, despite my motivation and my willingness.
Despite society's belief, I knew I could still contribute and have a use of some sort.

In the fall of 2022, I got back on LinkedIn (a social media platform) and dusted off my profile. I did everything I could to make my voice heard, to get my message read, and to make my motivation be seen. Also, I connected with many recruiters and sent hundreds of emails explaining my situation and asking for help to find a feasible job.

I was physically damaged, yet my mind was still intact.

My skills, capabilities, and knowledge have never been damaged; they've been here this entire time. And the most crucial matter is that my dream is still alive: to be apt to touch people's lives and help them through writing. I want to inspire and support other trauma survivors and chronic pain warriors by sharing my truth, experience, and lessons learned.

I have a disability; however,
I won't let it rule my life.
I won't let it hurt my soul.
I won't let it ruin my dreams.

No matter what you are going through, always believe in yourself, in your ability to overcome, and find a way to make the best of it. Even the slightest improvement makes a huge difference in your fragile life. You owe it to yourself and your loved ones to at least try and get better. Even if just a little bit, try to see for yourself if it works. What have you got to lose? You've already lost so much. It's time to get some of it back, right?

DROP TWO:

STORIES OF LIFE

The stories I share in this second
drop tell about meaningful topics
of everyday life. Aspects can
make or break your quality of life
if it's not going as you want.
Improving these aspects
will have a positive effect
on your life.

2.1 LOVE

Hopelessly seeking love.

As I didn't receive love and affection as a child, I desperately craved it during adolescence. Of course, the kind of love I was looking for was based on the only two examples I knew:

- the toxic, destructive kind
- the romance kind, like straight out of the Hollywood studios

It's safe to say my view and expectations of love weren't realistic or healthy, but I didn't know any better. I also believed that I couldn't be complete without it; finding love wasn't only a fantasy but an absolute necessity. I couldn't live by myself, and I needed someone to be with me to give me the support and strength I lacked, or at least that's what I believed.

Nobody showed me otherwise. Nobody ever told me you could find strength within yourself and that you don't need to depend on anybody else to achieve your life goals. On my desperate quest for love, I kissed a few frogs, hoping they would turn out to be a prince in shiny armor, defeating my demons and taking me away to greener pastures on his white stallion.

Yet no frog ever turned out to be anything but. How could they? My expectations were too high to meet. Nobody was up for it. If a boy was sweet, he was too sweet, thus uninteresting. If a boy was thoughtful, he was a doormat, and I stomped all over his little soul with my heavy baggage.

According to my unrealistic vision of love, love should hurt; it was intended that way. A boy should be out of reach, even playing with your emotions and sanity. That's the way it should be, right? Of course, that's wrong, so wrong, but I didn't know any better.

I was so fragile, so unconfident, and so easy to fool.

I was an easy prey.

Innocence lost.

Destruction of self.

Enter the narcissists.

Summer was just ending as I was about to turn seventeen. I was dating a boy I had met at a party a few days earlier. He was excited to have me meet his best friend. No one could have imagined what would happen the second that front door opened . . .

There are many ways to describe this kind of event:

- to be struck by lightning
- love at first sight
- the earth stood still

All of these describe an unpredictable event that comes out of nowhere and in which you're completely powerless. You can't do anything but experience it.

Yet, why is it we call this event love? A chemical reaction causes it; you don't even know the person in question, so how could you ever think this is love?

Because our body and mind fool us into thinking this is love.

- We feel it in our stomachs, with butterflies or some other ache.
- We feel it in our minds; we turn stupid and can't stop thinking about that person.
- And we feel it in our bones; our body reacts, giving us chills and goosebumps.

That's why we define that chemical reaction as love, and I believe it's the worst kind. Because you didn't get to know the person first, you aren't apt to make a rational choice, and you feel sick if you try to fight it.

I first realized this wasn't real love when someone asked me why I loved that boy, and all I could say was, "I honestly don't know." We were together for about two years at that point, yet because my inner self knew he was no good for me, I couldn't find one reason why I loved that person. But that freakin' chemical reaction was so hard to shake off. Despite all the evidence, the biggest one being the psychological abuse I underwent during those years, I still loved him.

I still see myself standing in front of the mirror, getting ready for school, noticing that my eyes were puffy because of the crying I did the night before. My eyelids were swollen, and I had to find tricks to hide them.

I could use some concealer, but it wouldn't mask it. Everyone at school could see it; all the teachers could see it, yet nobody ever asked me anything about it. I was a senior in high school by then; and that last year, which should have been a celebration of my academic career ending, became one of the saddest and loneliest years of all.

That's what happens when you love a narcissist:

- Your self-esteem takes a nosedive due to emotional abuse.
- Ending up in it so deep that you believe every word he says, even the meanest ones.

- You believe he is the only person in the world capable of loving you, so you cling on even more.
- And, you even believe you deserve the things he says and does; the alternative of losing him is unbearable.
- In the end you shut off your family and friends as they openly attack him and question your relationship.

Why are people attracted to things they know are bad for them?

It's about toxic love and nasty habits like fast food, smoking, or alcohol. Your mind knows it's bad for you, yet you are still drawn to it because it looks and smells good. The devil designed it well to lure people into temptation and make us like it.

So, I have to admit (not that I'm proud of it) that he wouldn't be the only narcissist I would date. It was as if one abusive experience wasn't enough for me, and I thought I deserved to be harmed some more, as love meant to be hurt. Right?

In Italy, we call it "*La sindrome della crocerossina,*" the Red Cross Syndrome. People want to save those in trouble; and aren't narcissists the perfect candidates? At first, they are charming and even seem vulnerable. They have apparent issues like drug addiction, and we believe we are the ones to save them from themselves. Our love will keep them safe. Sound familiar? But did it ever work? Did this story ever have a happily ever after? Mine didn't. The only happy part was freeing myself from them.

Another feature that should raise an immediate red flag is their constant lying and manipulating to get their way. It's all about them, never about you. It's about their needs, their wants, their pleasure. What you or anyone else wants doesn't matter to them. And they are so apt to make it seem like it's your idea. They get you to capitulate and back their idea; if not, they will make you feel guilty for being unable to love them. They're natural-born actors who can use any situation to their advantage.

Always remember that narcissists:

- are incapable of loving anyone but themselves;
- are only interested in themselves;
- are always lying and manipulating, even in their sleep; and
- are capable of far worse than you would ever think possible.

The only way they will ever leave you or let you go is if they already have other plans in which you don't fit in anymore. Their relationship with you is all about possession and being able to control you and your life as they please until they make other plans, meaning they have another target in mind. Make sure to recognize the red flags before they have you under their spell and break it off right that second. You don't want to be their new toy, their puppet.

The right time.

Timing is everything; it has such a significant impact on your life. If I had met my husband before my accident, he wouldn't have stood a chance, because he didn't match the toxic love I sought.

My accident was eye-opening; it made me realize that my idea of love wasn't love. When someone loves you, they are here for you; they don't walk away for no reason, and they definitely don't want to hurt you.

Love means caring, and when you care for someone, you don't think about harming them. The thought of that would make you sad. Caring means sheltering and protecting your love as if it were a wonder. Why would someone destroy such a gift with their hands? You would do anything to keep it safe and ensure nothing ever happens to it. You would even protect it with your own life if it ever came to it.

But I had to go through hell to realize all this. It's unbelievable, but it makes sense when you put it this way. And now that my eyes were finally wide open, I could see it too. After my accident, I not only worked hard on my physical recovery but also on my emotional recovery. Knowing I had put myself in this position was hard to take in.

For the first time since I can remember, I wasn't looking for love. I wasn't thinking of anyone but myself. It was the first time I put myself and my needs atop of the pyramid. And the great thing was that I learned to live with myself alone. I had been living alone for some years, but I never learned to be alone, as I was always part of a couple. This time, I was single and happy.

Here comes irony again, and you can feel it. For the first time, I wasn't looking for love, but then love came to me in the most unexpected way. I met my husband at a family gathering for a nephew who was about to enter this world. That was the first time I saw him; it wasn't love at first sight! Woo-hoo! I'm so happy about that as that is the worst kind of all. But there was something interesting about him that captured my attention, and we spent the entire day talking.

The next time I saw him was about a month later, when my nephew was born. But nothing happened, other than some laughs and a friendly chat. It was refreshing to have a relationship grow naturally, without forcing it or making it happen, as I often had in the past; and we know how that turned out . . . No, this time, no forcing it, no manipulation of any kind; I just let life take its course and see what would come of it, no expectations.

It wasn't until a week later that we went on our first date (which he denied being a date – an inside joke), and we haven't separated since. No, I'm not talking about fairytale cliché: "and they lived happily ever after." We had our fair share of struggles, but this relationship was different from the ones I had before. I wasn't trying to kiss a frog, hoping it would turn into a prince; I was kissing a man, period. That felt so good.

How did I know this was the real thing? He accepted me for who I am, as I did with him. It was the first time I didn't have to fake anything or hide some parts of my being because the other person didn't like it. I was finally free to be me, and that's everything. For the first time, I could be myself; no fake self or altered ego, just me. That is real love to me.

DROPS OF LIFE EXPERIENCE

Thirteen reasons to be proud and grateful.

It took a car crash to open my eyes to my past relationships and my idea of love.

As of this year (2023), thirteen years have passed since I met my husband. He's one of the good guys, trustworthy and present. I would have crushed him with my heavy baggage if I had met him before my accident. He wouldn't have stood a chance. Thank God for timing.

After thirteen years, I can share the secrets to lasting relationships with you. In my experience, these are essential aspects:

- Open communication: I mean no secrecy; you and your partner should be free to share everything, the good and the bad topics in life. You need to know where you stand in the relationship to feel safe.
- Honesty: Always be honest; don't sugarcoat it. Tell it like it is and trust your partner's ability to understand you.
- Reliability: You need to feel your partner's presence in the relationship; and I mean their emotional presence, not their physical presence. No shutting down or closing off. Be there for each other.
- Mutual respect: You don't need to agree on everything, but you must respect each other's point of view. You are entitled to have your own opinions without fear of judgment.

- Perseverance: No quitting in the face of adversity; no walking away as things get tough, and they will at some point. It's in adversity that you show your true colors. Stay, talk, and try to work things out.

- Empathy: Listen to each other and feel each other's aches and joys. Put yourself in your partner's shoes and try to understand their thinking.

- Patience: Things can take time, so be patient. Don't rush it or put any unnecessary pressure on each other. Give yourself the time you need.

A lasting relationship is work, not a walk in the park. When two different people try to build a life together, they commit. You need to keep a balance between two beings with different personalities and backgrounds. And keep in mind that all of this can change over the years. Like all living things, we keep evolving as humans; therefore, change and growth are inevitable. Still, you need to grow within your relationship, make necessary adjustments, and find common ground. Time and time again, as the years go on.

And yes, we did overcome quite a few storms as a couple and a family. Because you are both different people with your own points of view, you must keep that in mind and respect both parties.

Taking time for yourselves as a couple is vital to keep the spark alive. Spending time together as a family is essential to know each other as parents and guide your kids in the same direction. Every day, you choose your partner; you choose your family. Every day, you commit to them, and that's love too.

2.2 Growth

Opening up online.

Spending all this time home alone, I had one gateway to keep me in touch with the outside world, social media. I have always been very cautious, primarily online, as I don't easily trust other people. However, because of my situation, I went beyond my comfort zone and built an online community. At first, it was for my never-ending quest to find feasible work (more about this later) and to keep in contact with people.

But if I'm honest, opening up online is challenging. I don't fake it. I tell it like it is. One of the first things I noticed was how my words, the intention of my words, could be misinterpreted.

What would you prefer when it comes to getting to know people?

Would you want them to fake it and hide who they are?

Or would you like to know them for who they are and share their "ugly truth"?

When I was writing and sharing on social media about my struggle to find a job, someone said my words were negative. And they said I needed to be careful about my writing so as not to harm anyone. I was shocked, as anyone who knows me knows I am an incorrigible optimist, an idealist even, but never a negative person.

But I can't hide my reality; I can only describe my life, and sometimes, it's hard. Should I not mention it and keep up appearances? So, I thought to have AI respond to my question. I wanted to see if AI would describe my situation in another way, and this was the result:

"If a person should stay at home for 1.5 years without a job, the following could happen: first of all, the person would get bored and stressed [by] a lack of structural productivity. Without a source of income or a reason to get out of the house, the person wouldn't get the necessary activities to keep him mentally active and healthy. The second of these could be some financial issues. Having little to no income, the person should trust family or friends to keep his finances in order. Third of all, the person could become depressed because they would spend so much time alone, feel they have no added value to society, and [have] the feeling there is no light at the end of the tunnel."

Scary, right? Fortunately, this is not how it went for me, but it gives you a clear idea. It does objectively represent what I went through during that period when I was a full-time job seeker. Do you think AI's explanation sounds negative? Or did it just state facts?

It's hard to estimate what such a long period of struggle does to you, no matter how strong of a person you are. I am an introverted, highly sensitive person, so I am already completely out of my comfort zone by writing online about my experience for everyone to read. I'm a fish out of water on social media platforms. It's easier to share my experience with you, as I know you can relate. It's a comforting thought. I have to say thank you to the online community because it gave me a constructive activity other than my endless search for a job. It also gave me a figurative link with the outside world and with a part of society. It made me feel as if I was still part of an active society and its workers. And it gave me hope that I could contribute by sharing. In the process, I also learned, that it allowed me to continue to grow as an individual.

My writing and sharing will always be honest and reliable, but I remain a fish out of the water, so don't ask me to pretend otherwise or expect me to be fake or hide. All I need is the freedom to be myself. I've been silent for far too long, and now it's time to have my voice heard. Appreciate me for who I truly am or keep walking.

Ironic.

"It's like 10,000 spoons when all you need is a knife. It's meeting the man of my dreams and then meeting his beautiful wife" (Alanis Morissette).

Who didn't sing along with this song in the '90s? The singer described ironic events that every one of us knows all too well. Little did I know as a teenager that "irony" would occur several times in my life. Typical!

Here are some blatant examples of irony from my life:

1) After high school, I went to college to become an interpreter. Unfortunately, after two years, the person in charge told me that I was only allowed to continue as a translator, not an interpreter. They said my pronunciation wasn't perfect enough to work as an interpreter.

Oh no, I never considered working in a boring office job where you sit behind a desk every day. No way . . . The irony of this story? I've worked as a customer service representative and administrative assistant for over a decade; these positions were all office jobs that required me to sit behind a desk daily . . .

2) After my plans to become an interpreter fell through, I went to nursing school to help others. I had good grades and always passed; but then, the final year, when I finished my thesis, I found out I didn't pass it, so I couldn't graduate and needed to postpone my dream to go to Italy.

Oh no, I must wait another four months to redo my thesis. I will find a job in Italy and do that later on . . . Due to my accident, I could never complete my training, so I never got to graduate from nursing school.

3) In 2021, after years of "What-ifs" going through my mind, I realized I could still work as a healthcare professional since I had finished my first year in nursing school. So, I registered and immediately found a job as a nursing auxiliary at a retirement home.

Could my dream of helping others still come true after all these years? After barely two days, I was completely exhausted and had inflamed muscles. I went home crying from the pain and feeling like a failure.

What is the moral of the story? Life's a b*ch! Yes, sometimes it is, but mainly, do not postpone things, as life is unpredictable; and that makes it fascinating on one side, but it also makes your plans vulnerable on the other. You don't own time and don't control what happens in it either. Don't procrastinate; take action while you can.

> *Life is like a box of chocolates;*
> *you never know what you'll get.*

If you know what you want to do and believe in it, go for it right away.

Above all, please do not give up because of possible setbacks; see them as a test you must pass.

Nobody said you must go through this alone, reach out and find help.

Unfortunately, many things are out of your hands, but fortunately, others are.

Make your dreams come true without delay.

If it doesn't work out, at least you tried. There is no worse feeling than "what-ifs" running around your mind forever. Regret is omnipresent; don't do this to yourself.

Don't get caught up in distractions, doubt, or fear. Get up and move on.

There is always a way for you, even if the path may deviate from your initial plan, and it turns out to be an obstacle course.

The satisfaction at the end of the ride is your victory.

The feeling of accomplishment will be even more incredible and lift you higher.

Irony strikes again.

Irony strikes again? Oh no, it can't be . . .

In a previous section, I gave some blatant examples of ironic events from my life. History seemed to repeat itself.

Six years ago, I followed a training program to become a self-employed entrepreneur.

I thought I had found my mission on a professional level, created a website, and even printed business cards that are now in a cupboard.

Although I received many enthusiastic reactions, I lacked concrete potential working relationships, so I did not dare to take the step. I thought it was too much of a risk financially.

After all these years, I found myself in a search that became a never-ending story. And I've started to realize that I might have been right all along.

Had I been frightened by the fear of the unknown? Or maybe my lack of self-confidence?
Or was I scared to take the leap because of a lack of support in my immediate environment?

It was probably a combination of factors.
But how is the situation any different now?
In the end, the same fears still exist, especially now that the financial situation is even more delicate.
But above all, the realization that there's only a tiny chance to find a sustainable job through the regular job market has grown enormously.

Then I logged back into my website for the first time in about six years.
Yes, there it was.
How strange, as if time had stood still.

Could it be that I had already found my way six years ago?
Is working for myself the answer?
It's now or never. I know it this time; I'm sure of it.

Writing.

Drops of Life Experience

When I was just a little girl,
I lived in my safe haven; my imagination was everything to me.

I had so many stories running through my head, and there was only one way to stop them from interfering with my life. I needed to take pen to paper and write everything down.

As a teenager, I had a personal journal, which was a true lifesaver at times. I strongly recommend keeping a journal. There is no fantasy there, only real life without a filter.

My stories and my feelings still needed a port to land on. Sometimes, I wrote a few lines only; other times, I read entire pages.
The result? I started writing a novel at age eight and completed it when I was twelve.

I even illustrated it with my childish drawings and humor, directly taken from Leslie Nielsen. He cracks me up.

As I grew up, the stories in my mind began to take other forms. As I went to music school and learned to play piano, I wrote lyrics and even music.

In the end, being a teenager and all the drama I went through, my innocent and naive fantasy world was eclipsed by dark realism.

It was only a few years ago, when I almost burned out, that the urge to write down my thoughts on paper made a strong comeback.

Social media platforms allow me to have a voice and write about the arguments and topics that are dear to me. I no longer write sci-fi stories; I write the ugly truth taken directly from real-life events.
Hopefully, it can help others to gain some perspective.

I never want to stop learning; it keeps my mind powerful, alert, and young.

Writing is a natural way of sharing your thoughts without expressing them directly.
A blessing for an introverted, highly sensitive person like me, and I am so thankful for it.

The power of music.

Do you believe in the power of music?
I sure do!

Music has had a significant influence on my life.
It has always been there to lift me from a downfall, comfort me in times of need, and strengthen me when I feel faithless.

It's one of the only things that can impact my state of mind and change it swiftly.
One of the most significant examples was when my father passed away.
My mind said I should speak at his funeral; however, my heart couldn't.

Writing the text was the easiest part. It came quite naturally. However, the hard part was pulling myself together and making it through the reading without bursting into tears.

So, I did what I always do when I need some uplifting.
I put some music on really loud for hours.

Fortunately, we don't have direct neighbors, and I certainly wasn't going to get any sleep that night. The kids were staying at their grandparents' house. So, I had carte blanche.

What music did I choose?
Linkin Park
Metallica
Rammstein
Guns N' Roses

I listened to it up until the very last minute before we had to leave.
I was all wired up, feeling invincible, music vibes still running through my body and soul. They were giving me the energy I needed to go through with it.

And I did it.

I managed to read my text without crying. Thanks to music, I could say what my father meant to me and dedicate those words to him without hesitation.

Music has been a lifesaver and the healthiest medicine for me.

Who would have thought.

Those reading my posts online may already know that my life was struck by irony more than once. Just reading this book has taught you that much.

Well, this, too, is a fine example of some irony.

I am an introverted, highly sensitive person with quite a vivid imagination, and I don't need to add any extras, as I have films playing 24/7 in my head.

When I was a young child, I watched some horror films, which scared the hell out of me. Even though I haven't seen them since, the raw images, sounds, and screams are glued forever in my mind.

To everyone's surprise, and mine as well, I would never own a book from someone called King, first name Stephen. So, when my oldest son came into my room and noticed his book lying on my nightstand, he stood still, looking at me with a big question mark on his forehead.

He looked at me and said, "Mom, what is this doing here?"

"It's a book I'm reading for work."

Gosh, his eyes got big, and his mouth opened in shock.
He probably wondered what kind of job could ever need help from someone like King, first name Stephen.

"He's a book author, and this isn't what you think. It's like a guide for beginning writers." I could see some relief there, but even so, he still looked skeptical as he walked out of the room. I laughed.

I was skeptical, too, yet I discovered a great storyteller, which compelled me. We even had some things in common that created instantaneous links. To quote a few:

- the corner desk
- the need to work in a closed-off room, with the drapes shut
- the accident

I expected him to be such a grim, dark figure with only blood and abomination on his mind.

Yet I discovered a loyal family man who cares instead.
It reminds you not to judge a book by its cover or author.

Who would have thought.

Do you clean up your mess?

I've never been fond of cleaning.
I do it because I must, but I wouldn't say I like it.
But what happens if you don't? The rubbish gets worse, and you won't be able to see your interior design anymore. And that's what you care about. You spent so much time and effort to create the right atmosphere, the color scales, etc.

It's for the same reason we ought to clean up our writing.
Your message needs to be precise; therefore, you must cut what's unnecessary.
Just toss it out.

Details matter depending on the type of message you want to send.
Are you describing a scene of delict?
Are you providing your medical history?
Are you describing a most wanted person?

In those cases, every detail counts. You can't leave anything out because it's necessary.

Otherwise, keep it plain and simple.
"Cut to the chase."

You want to involve your reader, not put him to sleep.
Just keep it simple.

A second chance in life.

Almost fourteen years ago, life gave me a second chance.
I was living my life the only way I knew how; I was desperately chasing love to make up for the lack of affection in my childhood.

So, I met and kissed a few frogs, hoping they'd become my savior.
And the last frog took me to an unknown destination.
Right into a concrete wall. My seatbelt saved my life.

It was D-Day, as I call it—an eye-opener.
Through the months of rehabilitation, including physical therapy in the middle of the night,
my body and mind were so off track that I got insomnia.

I kept thinking, rethinking, and analyzing my entire life.
I had to find some meaning for this, so I reviewed everything I ever did in my mind.
When it struck me all at once, for the first time, it was crystal clear.
It was me all along.

DROPS OF LIFE EXPERIENCE

I was the one who chased the frogs.
I was the one who believed in lost causes.
And, I was the one who chose to be in bad relationships.

It's as if I thought I deserved it.
When someone tells you, time and time again, that you're not worth anything,
you end up believing it.
So, I believed I only deserved to be unhappy.
For me, love meant being hurt.

Well, all that changed as soon as I opened my eyes.
I would never have realized I was wrong if it hadn't been for my accident.
The words I grew up with were lies, and I deserved better.
Only a few months later, I was done walking with crutches.

I met my husband,
who was unlike anyone I had ever met before.
And I got to make my dream come true: I became a mom.
That's all I ever wanted.
I finally had the family I dreamed of as a child: loving and caring, built on trust and mutual respect.

Sure, we have our share of struggles.
Our life can be quite a challenge and even brutal at times.
But I wouldn't want it any other way.

I wouldn't change a thing, and I'm grateful every day.
So remember:
never give up,

never lose faith in you,
and never think you aren't worth it.

I went through hell and just kept going.
If I could, you could too.

Finally.

I finally got some of the answers I needed.
This is the fourth "research" book I've read about writing in the last week.
Even though every one of them had valuable and interesting advice about the craft, this one provided some of the answers I was looking for regarding one of my projects.

One project that's dear to me is writing my memoir (not to be mistaken for a biography).
I wish to come to terms with the events that struck my life, maybe even find understanding and peace.
I had some questions:
How do you get started?
What do you use, and what do you leave out?

Author William Zinsser explained the memoir writing process so well:
"*Your product is you; it's your story.*
Tackle your life with manageable chunks.
Make an honest transaction with your humanity.
Trust the small stories that still stick in your memory."

In the end, he also gave excellent advice on how to go about it. However, to find out, you'll have to read his book.

DROPS OF LIFE EXPERIENCE

My next read is already waiting on my nightstand.
But I will let this one sink in before I go on a new adventure.

That would be great, if only my mind would have a day off too.

I've always been curious.

I'm curious about everything in life.
We still know so little about many things in our frenzied, everyday lives. We walk by and hardly acknowledge their existence.

As I always wanted to look at those small things that have become invisible, I took my camera with me for a better view.

I never liked posed pictures of my loved ones.
I enjoy capturing moments when no one is watching.
Just steal an undisturbed instant of their existence.
Of course, my photo library mainly consists of family moments, kids fooling around, holidays, etc.

What I'm talking about is nature and its beautiful details.
Colors that are so magnificent that it's hard to grasp that they exist in our world.
But also textures, layers, and matter.

Every time, I'm amazed by what the camera shows me.
All I do is take a close image and adjust the lights and shadows.
That's it, just the subject in all its glory, without any photoshopping.

Please keep it simple and natural, the same as in writing.

And maybe next time you walk down the street, you'll take the time to look around at the world that surrounds you.

Let yourself be amazed by it all.

I had a dream.

I come from an immigrant family and was born and raised in Belgium.
My parents came from Italy and moved here in the '70s.

I didn't know a word of Dutch when I started school at two and a half years old. At home, we spoke Italian and watched a lot of French television.
But we spoke no Dutch whatsoever.

As you can imagine, going to school where they taught in an unknown language was quite a shock. I remember sitting there, just looking at everyone and feeling like an alien.
But even when I learned the language, this feeling of not belonging remained.

Kids started bullying me and telling me to go back to my country.
As a young kid, I didn't know what they meant. I was born and raised here. I didn't know any other country.
Of course, the other kids didn't know either. They were using the words they overheard from adults.

So, as I went home, I asked my mom what our country was, and she said we came from Italy.

Drops of Life Experience

My heart stopped.
So, it was true; the feeling I'd had since kindergarten of not fitting in was accurate.
Italy was *my* country!

I embraced this sense of belonging with open arms.
I held on to it so firmly that I finally had a country where I felt at home.
So, my entire childhood, I just had one thing on my mind; as soon as I graduated, I would go to Italy and get to know my country as a citizen, not a tourist.

I daydreamed about it for years.
When I graduated from high school, I continued my studies in college. So, I postponed my plans for a few years.
In the meantime, I went to Italy every chance I got.

Finally, as I was finishing nursing school in 2006,
I began to make my dream more concrete.
I went to Italy for two months, looking for an apartment to rent.

I was twenty-four years old and had no experience living alone. But I was sure of my dream.
Therefore, I would do anything to make it come true.
As August came, I had finished a sixteen-night summer nursing job, allowing me to fund my dream. I left with just one suitcase and got on a plane.

I remember my first night, and my electricity was yet to be activated, so there was no fridge, TV, or internet. Sitting there eating my dinner, a can of tuna with some bread, I realized the hard part was about to begin.

I had just enough money for two months' rent and living necessities. But that thought didn't scare me; it gave me the will to make my dream come true.

And as the deadline was about to hit in October, I found a job. The pay was not much, but it was a start.

I got to stay in Italy, and that was all I cared about.

The best gift I could ever receive came in April 2007, when I adopted a stray pup. I called him Dino.
He became my best friend, my guardian angel.
Even though he passed away in 2016, he's still with me, and I think about him every day.

I dreamed of going to my country and finally finding a sense of belonging. I ended up with so much more.

My love for Italy and a guardian angel are with me wherever I go.

I am still grieving.

How do I define grief?

The way someone tries to find inner peace after a sad, life-altering event.

Grief makes us think about someone passing away; however, it has a broader meaning.

You say goodbye to what's meaningful to you; you say goodbye to what you love.
In the end you say goodbye to what's dear.

A common factor in grief is going through different phases. Those phases are also used to make the process you are going through more understandable.

There is no guide, so the cycle of these phases varies from person to person.

It's a dynamic process.

To make it as clear as I can, this is my grieving cycle:

Denial: As I noticed the first symptoms, I couldn't face the reality I was in.
I wasn't ready for change and couldn't cope with another obstacle.
But, It was hard to accept that my life was about to change again.
It was hard to accept that I had to revise my plans.
It was hard to accept that I had to pause it all.

So, I tried to fake it, pretend not to see it, and go on as long as possible.

Anger: As pretending doesn't do the trick anymore, you face the ugly truth, and wrath takes over.
I was angry at the entire world, everybody and everything.
Moreover, I was in grave need of answers, as I kept asking: "Why?" "How?"
I was looking for something or someone to blame.

So, I expressed my anger by crying and acting out.

Fighting and negotiating: Once the eye of the storm passes, you calm down and brace yourself to face your new reality.
I coped by approaching this new event professionally.
And I coped by analyzing the situation and learning.
I coped by searching for solutions.

So, by facing the situation, I gained power and strength.

Depression: Once bargaining doesn't work and fighting doesn't help,
your belief in overcoming anything deflates like a balloon.
As a consequence, you fall off your high horse.
I felt powerless and was frustrated with the strong woman I thought I was.
And I felt tiny and vulnerable, like a bug about to be stepped on.
I felt I was losing myself, the "me" I was just a while ago.

So, I hid. I wanted to dissolve into thin air.

Acceptance: Once you find the exit within your dark tunnel and see the slightest ray of light shining through, you are open to accepting the change you're facing.
I became lucid and realistic and got rid of the bad.
Also, I became aware of the change and let go.
I became apt to deal with it.

So, I did what I could. I did my best and hoped it would be enough.

Drops of Life Experience

I said goodbye to the old me.
And I embraced the new me.

But I'm still getting to know her.
I'm still getting to like her.
I'm still discovering her.

She has something to offer too.
She has impressive qualities too.
She has the right to be, too.

I'm grieving still, but I have embraced the new me.
Therefore, I'm apt to cope with it and live my best life, despite the adversities.

If I can, you can too.

This is dedicated to all those coping with chronic illness and pain.

I wonder why.

We don't seem apt to recognize someone's worth, but we are always ready to overcome their flaws.

My father used to say:

Finché babbo è in vita, non sa fare niente.
Quando babbo non ci sarà più, sapeva fare tutto.

Meaning: As long as Dad was alive, he couldn't do anything. Once he passed away, he could do everything.

I never gave it much thought, as he said this often. Since his passing (almost three years ago),
I've come to realize he was right.

I have caught myself telling my kids anecdotes about their grandpa and how he was a great artist and could make anything from scratch.

I have caught myself telling my husband everything he could have helped us with inside the house, as my husband isn't a handyman. Dad got things done.

I can't grasp why I couldn't see this before.

Why is it that I see all these virtues now?
Why is it that I see all of his talents now?
Why is it that I see all of his worth now?

Honestly, I don't know.

There is no apparent reason I can think of.
But I think it's part of our flaws as humans. Therefore, we take things for granted.

What a pity.

On the bright side, we can change this.

I can change this starting right now.

You can change this as of now.

Let's take the time to focus on someone's worth.

Starting with ourselves is an excellent place to start. It will reflect on others as well.

When we're happy, we are willing to share our happiness too.

Mindset.

I have often referred to Bruce Lee because his life philosophy was so interesting.
His way of expressing his beliefs was so compelling.

He had such great charisma, an aura that surrounded his very being—not only while fighting but also while speaking.

He was gone too soon, like so many other great minds, yet he managed to leave a mark.

I often say, "It's all about mindset," as I am convinced of the truth in this simple concept.

Do you want to be healthy?
Or do you want to be happy?
Do you want to succeed?
Or do you want to evolve?

Meaning, you can do it if you set your mind to it.

You can find a video online for those who don't know him or his philosophy.
With a fragment from an interview where he explains his TAO water.

Everyday, simple words, but with much more relevance.

Therefore, those plain words become powerful.

Open your mind and be inspired.

To solve a problem.

To solve a problem, there are certain steps you need to follow:
- observe
- assess the situation
- decide what you need
- procure available tools for help
- proceed with solving the problem
- evaluate all the above and adjust where needed

Sounds logical.

Yet something important is missing: collaboration.

In business, we work in teams most of the time.
And it is so helpful to involve your team.

Even if you are apt to solve the issue on your own, working together has its benefits:
Teamwork brings diversity in ideas and approaches.
Competition increases creativity in your team.
Team players can share consuming tasks.

As a result, your solution will be a team win, motivating its members to do even better next time.

As the musketeers said, *"All for one, one for all. United we stand, divided we fall."*

Drops of Life Experience

Please give it up for those you can count on.

I hosted my radio show.

I spent much time alone in the '80s when I was a little girl. All I had to keep me company was my vivid imagination.

So, I entertained myself by making a radio show. I found one of the tapes between some old stuff at home. It was like getting into a DeLorean, leaving today's world, and instantly finding myself back in my old room.

I must have been about ten years old, tops.

So, I took my tape recorder and pressed two buttons to start recording.
I still remember the sound the tape made as it started to roll.

I listened to the tape with my husband and kids.
Initially, it was amusing, but I was amazed by the creativity the recording represented. Just by copying what I heard on TV and radio, I managed to host a talk show, invent my commercials, and talk with different voices and tones.

However, we all got silent when we stopped laughing at the absurdity of it all and started to listen to what I was talking about in the show.

However, the talk show was clever, dark, and sad. I remembered my show as fun and games, but now I realize it was serious and realistic.

The tape contained an interview with a physician about cancer. Followed by me interviewing smokers with cancer.

At that moment, I was shocked at the level of realism and adult conversation. I wondered why such a young child, in her own free time, would talk about such sad and life-altering events.

And I got emotional while I listened to my younger self.

I felt a deep sense of sympathy.
A deep sense of solitude.
A deep sense of sorrow.

I wanted to reach out and hug myself, as I felt like I needed it so much.
I hosted my radio show to create my dream, feel less alone, and be helpful.

And that is the essence of who I still am today: to help others, to make myself useful, and to create life stories so people can relate, feel less alone, and be understood.

I'll tell you why I write.

Why would someone in their right mind choose to do something so complex and, at times, unpredictable? That seems to be a recurrent question.

The answer is quite simple, obvious even to some. This isn't a conscious choice; it is just who we are.

I began writing as a young child, around eight years old. I wrote a fantasy story, as it was the only way to free myself from the daily aches.
My imagination saved me.

However, I never realized it at the time.
I never saw this for what this was.
Nor did I see this as a talent.
I never grasped this was it.

It took me forty-one years to finally realize it.
The blindfold finally came off, and for the very first time, I could see things. I will always be a writer.

Telling genuine stories about life.
Translating emotions into words.
And if I can motivate just one person during the process, that would be my biggest reward.

To be apt to touch people's lives, even if only for a short moment, is an honor. And I'm so grateful for it.

Do you like poetry?

I've wandered into new territory.

As a writer, my central theme is nonfiction.
I tell genuine stories of life and actual events based on my experience.

But I've participated in a poetry challenge for the past few weeks.

And what started as a challenge, what ought to have been a mere trial, turned out to be a discovery.

It turns out I like poetry.
And as it turns out I enjoy writing it.

I don't suck at it either.

Do you like poetry?
Have you ever tried to read it?

You'll find my poems in the next drop.

Remember that those were part of a daily challenge, a prompt, so there is an imposed word.
You'll find one in each title.

I'm a forever learner.

Curiosity is what keeps the mind young.
To be apt to look at the world through the eyes of a learner.
To see everyday things, eager to understand more about them.

I'm naturally curious, and I hope never to lose that feature.
It provides endless inspiration.

No matter what your aspirations might be,
let your curiosity drive you forward.

Ignite your will to learn.

Motivation is everywhere.

I often get motivated by athletes, as you need to have a powerful mindset to be a great athlete.

They often have humble roots, yet they're confident of their worth.
They show you how to go above and beyond to realize your dreams and how to get through physical and mental pain.

Drops of Life Experience

I often refer to the quote below. It comes from Rocky Balboa, a famous fictional boxer from the past.
I heard it in the *Rocky* movies, which I like very much.

"It isn't about how hard you hit; it's about how hard you can get hit and keep moving forward."

Adversity makes you stronger if you keep going, no matter what.

Burnout.

A concept I've gotten to know in the past.
I compare it to sinking in quicksand when asked how it feels. You don't even notice it's happening to you at first; it progresses slowly, and suddenly, you feel like you're sinking more and more every day. The more you struggle and resist, the more you'll sink.

Stop before it's too late, or you'll go under. Just stand still in the present (the "here and now").
Only when you give in to the situation and embrace it will you be able to deal with it.

Don't wait till you're drowning to reach out for help.
Asking for help is not a sign of weakness; it's a sign of courage.

Brick by brick.

Instead of dropping what's negative in your life, you can build upon what's positive.
In the end, you'll have more positive things than negative ones.

Brick by brick, day after day.

I applied the same philosophy when I endured a traumatizing period as a teenager. At that time,
I felt like my whole life was a house of cards, so fragile that it could crash into pieces at any moment.
If you would only touch one of the cards, it would be the end of it.

So, I focused on the good things and how small they could be. I went to sleep each night, thinking the next day would be better.

Each day was a new beginning, a fresh start, a unique chance.
I am never looking back, only forward.

You never forget what's happened.
However, you can learn to accept and decide to keep going and hope for a better future.

That you *can* do.

2.3 Work

Where is the glitch?

During my months as a job seeker, I read articles about how to get job seekers started.
What verbs did they use? Obligate and restrict.

That is an interesting and ironic choice of words since my disability is one of the reasons for my unemployment.
What strikes me most is that both verbs are negative and restrictive. The first wants to take away your right to choose, and the other wants to take away your financial support.

So, I ask myself, *What is their intention in the end? What do we, as a society, want to achieve?* Because, by stigmatizing and belittling people, you can never expect anything positive to come out of it.

This topic affects me personally, which I, unfortunately, know a lot about in the first person.
Every time I had a conversation with a recruiter or an employment agency, it struck me that they asked about my work experience and skills. Still, they never asked how I ended up in this situation and how it affected me as a human being. Shouldn't this be the starting point for a constructive conversation to tailor the approach to the person seeking a job?

As if there were a checklist of "questions to ask" or a one-size-fits-all approach that recruiters can copy/paste on each of us.
That's absurd, right?

Too often, we hear about numbers, statistics, and specific groups, but we forget about the essence. This regards people of flesh and blood with baggage of experiences and obligations toward themselves, their loved ones, and society but also with emotions, fears, expectations, etc.

Do recruiters want to tackle unemployment efficiently?
If they do, they should start with the essence and focus on the *person* standing before them, not the candidate.

Mama Manager.

If you introduce yourself to someone you're meeting for the first time, you usually use your job, function, or title to introduce yourself.
But why are we doing this, to begin with?
Of course, your job says something about you, but it doesn't say anything about who you are. A lucky few have managed to land their dream job or mission, but many are content with what they were offered and try to make the most of it—the typical work to live.

Yet, what do you need to reply when you are a job seeker?
If you introduce yourself as "I'm unemployed," or "I'm looking for a job," you will get that look of "Ah, so you're sitting at home doing nothing." And I know that look all too well . . . so embarrassing and frustrating because you are much more than that.

That is why I wrote in my current work situation that I am a mama manager because, in practice, this best reflects my daily life. Because one thing's for sure: I don't know anything about doing nothing!

A household can be compared to running a non-profit organization. Make sure to organize, make plans, problem-solve, and administer. You need to have an eye for people management, and you must see that everyone has what they need to practice their jobs or hobbies. Sending e-mails and doing some calls, follow up on their schoolwork, and care for the family's four-legged pals.

You are the central hub of your household; you take care of yourself and others, and you should be proud of that. So, why should you diminish yourself by saying you're unemployed when meeting new people? You are more than a technicality that says nothing about you and your life's responsibilities. Be proud of what you do.

Ghosting.

Ghosting is a phenomenon that doesn't just occur when dating.

It's one of the most frustrating things you can encounter as a job seeker. And I did.

It affects not only the applicant but also your person. You can't keep the two separate because you don't know what this behavior is about in the end.

The phenomenon usually occurs in the same pattern:

- First contact with the recruiter went great; it was positive.
- The recruiter complimented your skills.
- The recruiter believed you had potential and endless possibilities.

- The recruiter made you feel like they found the diamond in the rough they'd been waiting for.
- The recruiter promises to find the right job for you.
- The recruiter leaves you with expectations and dreams; you think the moment has finally arrived when someone sees you for what you're capable of.

Then comes the cold shower, but unfortunately, awareness does not come as pouring rain, where you are presented with the raw reality. No, your understanding is dripping in, little by little, which hurts even more.

Next comes disbelief and the endless questions:

- Was it because of me as a person?
- Were they deterred by my work disability?
- Am I too old for this job market?
- Does it have to do with my family name and migrant roots?
- Is my motherhood a stumbling block?

I'm always asking my peers for constructive feedback; no matter its content, you can learn from it and grow from it as a person and a professional.

It is beyond my logic why people behave in such a way when dealing with others—especially with those already in a vulnerable position. During such conversations, you often expose a part of your heart and soul to someone you don't know. You put your destiny in their hands.

So, let this be a learning moment for those who have behaved like this, whatever the reason.

Now that you know the other side of the story, you can commit to stopping this from now on.

No one benefits from this. On the contrary, it's uncalled for and harms already fragile situations.

Data vs. reality.

Earlier, I shared my experience with the phenomenon called ghosting, which I experienced as a job seeker.

I explained the questions I often asked myself in that situation:

- Is it because of me as a person?
- Am I too old for this job market?
- Is my disability an obstacle?
- Maybe it's because of my name/migrant roots?

As a coincidence, I came across an interview on the evening news regarding a study made in my country about the primary thresholds for job seekers. I heard that my above assumptions constitute three of the four most common reasons for discrimination worldwide and, therefore, where I live.

To test it out, I took the time to pour my applications into a small-scale chart. To make it relevant with regard to the ability to investigate discrimination, I chose to divide the graph into four types of responses recruiters gave to my applications:

- No response received whatsoever.

- I was ghosted.
- A response that comes across as a ready-made copy/paste reply, where the employer kindly rejects you without telling you the reason why.
- A response with concrete feedback that effectively tells you why you were rejected.

I had only taken the last trimester of 2022 to do this, the period in which I started applying consistently every day and is, therefore, the most representative. Of course, out of respect for privacy, I didn't mention any further details on this chart, and it's completely anonymous.
Additional information: I only received three interview invitations from these applications.

My search went on, but what conclusions can we draw from this? The fact is that discrimination cannot be proven because, of course, no one explicitly states this as a reason. It remains a guess that has a possible negative effect on my search. But it remains a possibility. Therefore, I'm even more powerless if this were to be the case. What can you do when dealing with discrimination of any type if nobody owns up to it?

I was trying to make them see things differently.

I have always liked to use metaphors to explain a situation more clearly. This is one of those metaphors.

A soccer coach and his technical director talk about hiring new talent.

"Coach, I looked at the competition's highlights, and my eye fell on a talent with great potential."

"Really? New emerging talent?"

"This player has swum through all the waters. CA is a midfielder with much experience, who sees the game and knows what needs to be done to score."

"Much experience? Do you mean old? That's not what I have in mind. Where did she play?"

"Not old, but wiser. What makes CA able to take the younger players under her wing? She can support and guide them. CA has played at some of the best international clubs."

"Some. So, with more than one? Why did she often change clubs?"

"At the first club, CA was firmly in the core, but due to a transfer, she could not stay. CA was lent to clubs in need, where she always came in to strengthen the team. This means that CA is multipurpose and can take on multiple tasks. Budgetary reasons stood in the way of a takeover."

"Hmm, a very experienced midfielder who can support others on the team and is multipurpose? Tactically, I think it's an interesting move. The person for the job. I'm curious; take care of it."

Would you give CA a try if you were a recruiter?

It's such an odd way to be approached.

When I was an active job seeker, I was contacted by recruiters on a frequent basis.

But in this new way, I asked myself serious questions.

I got a call, and as soon as I answered, I heard an automatic tape starting to roll: "We have a job that might interest you. If you're interested, press one . . .".

So, for starters, how can you effectively know if you're interested in that job based on this? You don't know anything . . .

My sense of duty wanted me to press one. You never know. You don't want to miss an opportunity.

But what happens then? I would again receive an automatic taped message, saying that I was put on hold: "All representatives are on the line; please wait a moment."

My immediate reaction was disbelief and frustration: *Are you kidding me??*

The agency contacted me because they wanted to discuss a job opportunity, and then I had to wait for them to come to the phone. And eventually, I would get someone on the line who didn't know who I was or why I was calling . . .

No, I object with force!

I find this approach disrespectful, and I don't understand this way of "helping" job seekers.

What do you want to achieve with this? Is it just about quotas or targets? Do you want to contact as many job seekers as possible in one day, and it doesn't matter if you helped them effectively?

I thought the intention was to help job seekers find work.
All those promising slogans turn out to be pure marketing in such cases.
Once the credibility is lacking, you lose me as a "customer" anyway. I may have been a job seeker at that time, but I'm still a person who has values and is worthy of respect.
Work ethic and professionalism are part of this.

That's how they taught me when I trained as a customer service representative; and that's always been one of my credos—both personally and professionally. I commit myself completely; otherwise, I do not start something.
Maybe it's worth thinking about.

Let's be clear: I'm not saying all recruiters are the same. I was lucky to find a few capable and reliable recruiters on LinkedIn. A special thanks to Elke Horemans and Annik Lamin, who took the time to get to know me and took my story to heart, which I could count on in those days, even when I didn't ask for anything. People like them are the exception that confirms the rule.

A search.

New Year's is an excellent time to look at achievements.
So, in January '23, I focused on the recruiters who gave feedback on my application.

Why wasn't I recruited for those jobs?
1) "We chose candidates already working for the organization."

    They want an employee who requires as little time and energy as possible.

Although I understand this, it didn't give me hope for future job openings.

So, only the same people get a chance to work there? How about offering everyone an opportunity?

2) "We require a bachelor's degree for this function."

So, they do not mean "equal by experience" or "bachelor's level of thinking and working," regardless of whether I had the required skills.

Again, there is no room for other opportunities as long as this is the company's recruitment ideal.

I suspect it is because of government funding. Could the government do anything about this?

3) "We don't want to make any exceptions regarding hybrid or remote work."

They wanted me to be present at the office every day as any employee.

I thought this response was strange, as the person I would replace worked from home one day a week. The interviewer said nothing negative about this during the interview.

To attach importance to the continuous presence in the office, would this have to do with some form of control and mistrust? Just like they require a sick note when you call in sick?

The feedback was plausible, but unfortunately, these are not pain points I could change myself. I felt powerless in my search for work, yet again.

Hopefully, employers will make more effort on job design or job crafting. To see a job seeker as a person with a unique mix of personality, experience, and potential.

Step away from the static and theoretical job description.
Ask yourself, "What traits and skills should my ideal colleague have?"
A fresh start isn't a new place. It's a new mindset.

Job design.

As the mindset didn't shift from their side, I decided I had to do it.
I finally launched myself as a freelance solopreneur on March 1st. I didn't see any other way to have work. But isn't this also an example of job crafting or job design?

A purpose is terrific, but the main reason for this transition to independent status remains not finding work in the regular labor market.

Helping others remains the essence of who I am, but no longer as an employee—a slight nuance but with significant differences in practice. Especially on the administrative and financial levels, if you focus on risks and responsibilities, I think it is great that many young people from Gen Z are already launching themselves.

It took me so long. But better late than never; no regrets, right?

Job crafting only goes so far, so I have changed the form to create more opportunities for me to work. But the offer still comes from the same fishpond, namely the regular labor market.

And if the pond is the same, so are the fish to be caught.

Irony strikes again? No, this time, it's pure realism. The most significant pain points I have encountered for years are more persistent than I thought, but where there is a will, there is a way.

If you do not ask for change, then it will not come. Hence, a warm call to business leaders, customers, and clients here to be more open to letting their employees work from home. It increases productivity. Flexible hours allow us to plan and manage work efficiently.

A happy person who feels understood and appreciated will perform better and pay you back with loyalty.

Sustainable cooperation is achieved. It's a *win-win*.
Give it a chance; others show it can be done.
My fishing rod is ready.
Where's that fish?

Has anything changed since I became an entrepreneur?

Not much; working freelance closely resembles being a job seeker:

- Networking
- Registering on work platforms
- Active job searching
- Collecting rejections

But there is a vast difference. My mindset has changed not only me but also the outside views!

What a difference in response when someone asks, "What are you doing in life?"

When I answered, "I'm a job seeker," that meant sitting at home, doing nothing . . .
But when I answered, "I'm a freelancer," they responded, "Oh wow, that's great!"

It's weird because I am still the same person, and in practice, the two things mean the same thing, yet the reaction is entirely different. Or should I say, people's perception?
It makes me feel completely different; and it shows in everything I do, even in my writing.

There were those who did not understand me when I said that I didn't want to wait for the second quarter to pay less social contribution. I also told them that I didn't want to start with the government method and keep wearing the stigma of unemployment for another year. I couldn't bear it.

Do those people understand me now?
Everything is not about money, even if it is an essential factor in life, especially if you've been losing revenue for months. But your mindset makes you feel better about yourself, resulting in more energy, positivity, and productivity.

Sometimes, you have to give something up and take a risk to achieve something great.

Such a new experience.

Two weeks after I started as a freelancer, my first happy moment occurred when I received an email from government authorities, confirming that I was no longer registered as a job seeker!

Whoa!

What a fantastic feeling of freedom. The strings were finally cut.

The stigma called unemployment that I was wearing unfairly had weighed so heavily on me, especially if you know I moved heaven and earth to turn the tide.

Did I start at the bottom of the ladder?

I'd say somewhere in between because this is an unknown territory with many possibilities.

As a multipotential, this is a delightful playground.

You can do all sorts of things, depending on your skills and experience.

You can also provide variety by doing various small assignments.

I have always been curious and eager to know and understand new things.

So, this is the ideal setting for me to learn new things and feel the necessary challenge that creates positive stress. It's never too late to know that's a fact!

And no lesson is too small or insignificant, as long as you find value in it.

Self-development is as essential to human beings as breathing.

DROPS OF LIFE EXPERIENCE

My home office: a desk, in the corner.

An exclusive look behind the scenes of my cozy home office—a small corner that I have appropriated in our bedroom. But with goodwill, we transformed it into a pleasant and practical workplace.

When I told my boys I would work as a freelancer, they spontaneously started making drawings. Super sweet, right?

The puzzle in front of me is the last one I put together during my unemployment period; it's a puzzle from a magical bookstore. The image has lovely little details hidden in it; I find others whenever I look at the pieces.

I got the photo frame on my desk from my husband and children when I returned to work for the first time after my burnout period. Since then, it has had a fixed place on every desk where I worked.

The original thing is that there is a voice message to listen to through a button at the bottom of the frame. And what happens? The message sometimes plays spontaneously without me pushing it.

Then, out of nowhere, you hear the voices of my boys saying all together, "*Ti voglio bene!*"
That immediately puts a smile on your face.

And what does your workplace look like?

What is talent?

If I read a job description demanding "experience," does this include talent *and* life experience? But what is talent, or rather, what is meant by it?
Most of the descriptions say that this is innate.

What is life experience?
What you have learned in your daily life—the knowledge you have already acquired.

Is this knowledge less valuable than what you are taught during a training course?

There are many reasons why some don't pursue higher education:

- Some don't have the financial resources.

- School format is not for everyone (think of well-known successful school leavers).

- Some have cultural upbringings with a focus on work.

- Some are thwarted by life.

Full-fledged reasons, right?

So, why should we value talented people with life experience less than those taught in school? What matters? That the candidate has demonstrable knowledge, or how the candidate acquire this knowledge?

Knowledge is knowledge, no matter where it comes from. Focus on the essence, not the form!

Everyone deserves a fair chance; you all need to work.

I am tired but happy.

It's April. I have already been working as a freelancer for one month. And my first two projects are about to be completed successfully. The first payments have already arrived, and although I began to work very modestly, it feels so good to earn a living without help.

As a job seeker, you feel frustrated because you didn't choose that situation.

Now I have to work twice as hard for less money, but the feeling of pride is all the greater and more intense.

As an employee, we've all had days in which we were not at our usual top level in performance, having difficulty getting through the day. However, as long as you were present in the office, you still received your salary, despite your lack of productivity.

It's a luxury when you think about it.

But it is difficult to respect your boundaries; I have always been a workaholic; it's who I am, as I have always enjoyed performing at work. So, now that I work remotely, I have already faced this side of myself a few times. It will always be a pain point for me.

Are you serious? Are you back in your old patterns?

There's high pressure to perform, which I certainly experienced. But there's also a sense of recognition, which I have longed to have for so long. It's awesome to have an employer who is satisfied with your work and takes time to praise your work making you gain confidence in your abilities.

Afterward, the search can go on to the next assignment. The next project, how exciting!

One of the perks of working from home.

Do you know that colleague who stays behind at their desk during their lunchtime, saying they will join you in five but never end up joining you?

Yep, that was me—the workaholic eating lunch at her desk or skipping lunch.

Now that I'm working from home, I'm taking more breaks throughout the day and learning to take time to eat lunch. It sounds silly writing this, and I bet it sounds silly reading it, too, but it's an evolution for me.

To correct this habit, I take time to prepare and eat lunch. This is mostly healthier, as I'm eating more slowly, but it is also less expensive and eco-friendly, as I check my fridge for fresh products and keep them from going bad. It's a win-win.

I'm a Nerd. I know.

Yep, I admit it. I'm a nerd.
I enjoy learning new things, and it can be pretty addictive.

One of the good parts of being a freelancer is learning new things continuously.
Jumping from project to project, from challenge to challenge, is so satisfying.

Drops of Life Experience

Even between jobs, I can explore different things to gain more experience and increase my possibilities for paid positions.

How? By volunteering.

No, I don't mind, as the geek in me is being nourished, and in the end, it's an investment in my future work. And in my personal growth as well.

What I learned today, I will be able to use tomorrow.

And in between all this, I return to my passion for concrete hobbies: putting puzzles together and building LEGOs.

It's so great to see the result of what you've been working on, but it is also fun to see the evolution day after day as every piece, every block, finds its place. I love it. And sometimes, you might be surprised by a subliminal message, this time straight out of the brilliant mind of Master Yoda.

"Do. Or do not. There is no try."

It's as simple as that; there's no need for much thought or adding lip.

I can't believe it.

Sometimes, you are amazed at how things can turn out. In the meantime, it's been almost two months since I leaped into entrepreneurship. I came from a path filled with obstacles, where I, as a jobseeker with a working disability, was confronted with various challenges.

Two issues seemed to be the most difficult to overcome: working from home and working part-time.
The same challenges are still present despite my giant leap.
But what have I experienced in the meantime as a freelancer?

I have seen firsthand that part-time work per se no longer has to be an essential condition, as long as I can manage my hours. Which, of course, is a significant advantage, a game-changer, in my case.

I can manage my time independently if I get clear expectations from the client toward the deadline and clear guidelines. Of course, we are talking about flexible hours, not 9 to 5, which I must adhere to. Working full-time in set hours is still a no-go for me.

How do I proceed while paying attention to my work disability?
I take regular breaks, so I can always recover enough, and I listen to my body.
I continue working as soon as the battery is charged. I have caught myself at the computer, still working at 10 p.m.

But going to sleep on time is still a crucial thing; I won't skip that! I need to go to sleep before 11 p.m.

The same goes for the weekends when I must balance work and family.

Runners experience the "runners high," and, similarly, I experience the "workers high," especially after I have successfully completed something and feel proud of myself.

I'm a nerd; I know.

Communication.

What's the secret of lasting relations?

I have worked in the field as a nurse auxiliary, behind the scenes as a customer service representative, and I'm in a marriage. In life, all relationships, whether business or personal, are based on communication.

Communication enhances
- ✓ understanding
- ✓ agreement
- ✓ trust
- ✓ clarity

It also prevents
- ✗ misreading
- ✗ disagreement
- ✗ uncertainty
- ✗ ambiguity

Even if only one of the above elements are missing, it could end any relationship.

Communication needs to be
- ✚ true
- ✚ engaging
- ✚ tailored
- ✚ definite

It's essential that all parties involved feel safe and welcome.

Therefore, communication has to be respectful toward all engaged parties. There is no hierarchy; we're all on the same level. Mutual respect is to be asserted. Never wait for issues to occur before you decide to reach out; prevention is essential. You need to be proactive by keeping track and taking a hands-on approach.

And maybe the most underrated element of all, show you care! To care is to be empathetic; that matters because, in the end, we all want to feel understood.

It's essential to have specific rules while engaging with others. Discuss some guidelines; however, don't set boundaries. Don't exclude people, but be accessible.

Don't forget the essence of communication. For good communication, as stated above, hands you the key to get through the door. And once you're in, it's all up to you!

Some recognition.

What a wonderful surprise it was when I received an email from Upwork (a work-from-home platform) stating they rewarded me with a top-rated badge.
It was such a wonderful feeling to see some recognition for my work.

Sure, the timing was everything, as I was in the right place at the right moment.
I had only registered for one day and received two requests to send my application.
And I was accepted for both jobs!

I was grateful for this chance to get me through the door, but it was up to me from then on.
Therefore, I worked hard to show what I was capable of—what I was all about.

I'm so curious to see what other opportunities will follow next and am so happy I finally took a step toward a freelance life; even though it didn't happen until I was forty-one, it's never too late to follow your dreams.

As your dreams never go out of style.

If I can do it, you can too.
It's all about mindset; you've got the power to change things.

2.4 Parenthood

Motherhood.

One thing I have always been sure of is my desire to be a mom.

Whenever I was asked as a child, "What do you want to be when you grow up?" I couldn't answer it.

But I was sure of this. I have always wanted a family of my own, a white house with a picket fence, and a backyard that would feel like a park—a place where I would feel safe and loved.

Maybe the lack of such a home in my childhood made me dream ahead to accomplishing this. Whether biological or not, motherhood is not an instinct you are born with. At least, this is not the case for everyone. I witnessed that firsthand.

It's a bit weird if you think of it; you need a driver's license to drive a vehicle or be a certain age to drink alcohol. Yet anyone can get pregnant and give birth to a child. And it is assumed that you will take care of your child. And often, people around you close one eye and one ear if they see something is not going well inside the home. Domestic abuse isn't that subtle, yet people won't speak up or report such events, even if they are sure of what is happening between those walls.

When you grow up like I did, you grow up fearing to reproduce that behavior in your kids. Why? Because it's all you've ever known "parenting" to be. It's been your example for years. You've never seen otherwise, except for movies on TV. That fear showed its ugly head right after my youngest was born. I didn't want to hurt my kids, but my instinct told me to act aggressively.

How often did I hide in the bathroom to cry it out, get myself together, and wait till that ugly head disappeared? How often did I call my husband, asking him to calm me down, as fighting that ugly feeling within me was so complicated? Still, I could hear her voice and words, and the tone . . . that tone was the worst.

And I knew hiding and running away from those situations wasn't the answer. Therefore I needed an external perspective to help me out of this mental loop I was stuck in. That was the first time I saw a therapist regarding what happened in my childhood. And it was long overdue. My husband came along a few times, as I felt it was essential for him to understand some of the difficulties I was facing and the "why" to some of my reactions. Those sessions helped us out a lot, and it did help me defeat that ugly head! Whenever it tries to show up again, I laugh at it. It has no power anymore.

I'm not that child anymore.
And I'm not her.
Now I'm a mom myself, and I do love my kids.
I don't want to hurt my kids, ever.

The truth is that no one is born with a manual. You will find out as you grow both in years and in insight. You gradually realize that the concept of parents does not consist of the books of pedagogy.

They are people of flesh and blood, each with shortcomings. That doesn't make it all right, but it helps to put things into perspective.

To give it a place, gain some understanding.
No, it wasn't up to you.
No, it wasn't your fault.
No, you couldn't have done anything else.
And now that I have children of my own, I can only do one thing: my best!

And do this every day, over and over again.
Has my childhood dream come true? Yes! But motherhood and its challenges have just begun.

Values.

When my kids bring their school results home, I always pay more attention to what their teachers say about them. I look for details about how they act in school, how they contribute in class, and how eager they are to learn.

We can all get good grades, but that doesn't tell me who you are. Maybe you are just a quick learner, have a good memory, or are just lucky.

However, your attitude reflects your values in life.

Are you helping others?

Are you focused?
Are you selfish?
Are you able to adapt to every situation?

Most of those are aspects of your character that you were born with. The ones that can't be taught or unlearned.

However, values can and *should* be taught.
Especially as a parent, it's a priority, my priority.

When a teacher says, "You've raised a good person with healthy values," well, that's the most beautiful thing someone could say about my child. I couldn't be more proud, which means I've succeeded as a mompreneur.

Bullies.

Being the mom of two wonderful kids with physical disabilities, I know the fear of them getting bullied at school. But I am trying to make them resistant to it or at least give them the tools to cope.
I'm working on taking away the power those cowards would try to use over them psychologically.
Because those bullies are not more intelligent or better looking. Their cruelty and insensitivity are just the specter of their unhappiness.

I explained to my kids that if someone should insult or mock them, they must remember that those bullies are the first to be unhappy. Because happy people do not even think about mistreating others, bullies aren't giants to be defeated but kids just like them who feel bad inside.

We must regain power from those who want to hurt us by defusing their influence, making them harmless.

Integrity.

Money, money, money, is all I read about these days.

I have been consistent on LinkedIn for about six months, and one of the things that often comes back is "money." People talk about how you can earn it, preferably as quickly as possible.
Some even put this in their headline, where they make big promises to their customers or followers.

Are there really people who want to make money fast, no matter what? The more, the better? No matter the cost?

Then I feel like an alien, a fish out of the water again.
I am no stranger to this world and know that you need money to live, but I do not make it a goal to pursue money. My life doesn't revolve around it.

Money does not determine my life or who I am.
Values do, and even though they don't bring me material things, they make me feel richer.
And this is such a hard lesson to teach my kids who live in this society where they want it all and want it now. It's so different from the reality I grew up in, where most of my toys were secondhand.

I'm not materialistic, and I try my best not to spoil my kids and make them see that things are only things. Material things are not what matters; it's the people in our lives that matter, and our health matters too. Those things are priceless and irreplaceable. Yes, money can make your life somewhat more manageable, but money can't buy relationships or health. The best things in life are free of charge.

I am content with what I have, and that is extremely valuable. I hope I'll be able to teach them that, too.

School gives me stress.

My son said this to me while we checked his weekly school schedule.

I have always had fond memories of my school days, as I am a nerd and just liked learning; but first and foremost, school was my only break from the toxic situation at home, so I looked forward to it every school vacation and every weekend. My eldest son is eleven years old and is still in elementary school.

If he is already experiencing stress while the "real" work has yet to begin, what will it be like next September, once he takes the big step to secondary school?

You feel powerless as a parent, as a mother in my case, because you want your child to be happy and protect them from any negative feelings.

I know like no other what it is like to live with stress, and I almost burned out a few years ago because of it . . . I would never have thought that my son would be confronted with this at such an early age.

School time should embrace childlike innocence and carefreeness; it should be fun, playful, and at the same time, make you learn without stress.

September is at the door; I cross my fingers for him.

Be inspired.

This is the second time I have had to explain my reading choice, another book I heard of on LinkedIn, to my children this week.

I was a bit reluctant at first when I saw the title.
The word "steal" is provocative, which is what made me read it in the end.

Of course, the author doesn't mean you have to steal anything. He talks about getting your inspiration from what you experience in the world.

We can draw inspiration from the world around us:

- what we see
- what we read
- what we listen to

We all start by imitating:

- what we like
- what we admire
- what we believe is excellent

As the author says, nothing is original.
What makes it different is being yourself and adding your touch of personality.

We can all read a recipe; however, we make it our own by adding the spices we love.
Some like extra salt; some like extra basil, and some like extra pepper.

And that little extra makes it your own story.
It makes it an original, after all.

So, it's okay to "steal" with your eyes; add that little extra that makes it your own.

Create what you love.

Today, we celebrate.

Another milestone in a boy's life.

Another milestone in a parent's life.

Another milestone in a family's life.

Today, we celebrate my firstborn's solemn communion.

We join together with family and friends on this beautiful summer's day,
it's important to share, support, and be there.

In such joyful times, we appreciate the good we have received in life.

It is important to be thankful, to remember, and to witness.

Today, we celebrate as my oldest son sets foot on the dawn of the next chapter in his life.

2.5 Change

Togetherness.

It's the most beautiful time of the year.

Christmas is my favorite time of the year, and it always has been since I was a child. With a problematic childhood with many toxic conflict situations, Christmas was the only day in the year when it felt as if everything was possible. Everything was different from any other day of the year.

As an adult, I have not forgotten my inner child, and I look forward to this special day. Regardless of the difficulties I'm facing at that time, I continue to believe and hope in that magical atmosphere.

As a job seeker, however, this period brings a great void, as I couldn't share this holiday period with colleagues. Because even if you and your coworkers do not always see eye to eye, at Christmas, you put all your differences aside; and everyone appears to be friendlier, more committed, and more open to each other.

You get to know people from different aspects, and you might even make new friends. To increase the feeling of togetherness, I organized (when I used to be employed) a secret Santa.
It was for those who wanted to bring a small token of kindness to another colleague for a reasonable budget. You need to be creative without embarrassing anyone because it

is anonymous, but it allows everyone to make a gesture and receive something in return. The mystery of the Secret Santa identities would always be an excellent topic for conversation at the coffee machine.

My wish is that this tradition lives on without me, and someone dares to take the step for others. You never know what someone else is going through in their life. This could be the only light in the dark for someone. It is the time of connection, of togetherness.

No one should ever spend the holidays, or any ordinary day, alone.

I see you.

This quote will immediately resonate with film lovers, but I do not use it to advertise the movie. It is a significant quote when you look beyond its literal meaning. The quote emphasizes the importance of seeing someone for who they are as a person, as if you could look at others with Superman's gift of X-ray vision (without the nasty body parts, of course). Only to see your inner self.

For those who have been invisible for a long time, like me, suffering from an invisible condition, we long to be seen. The irony is that if you feel invisible, you will make yourself even more invisible by isolating and shielding yourself from the outside world.

At the same time, you need to be seen and receive sincere attention.

Chronic pain is something I've been living with for years, and I haven't had a day without pain since 2009. Beyond the physical pain itself, I still find the disbelief from others to be hurtful. Or rather their ignorance, their disinterest.

When someone sneezes, we are taught in childhood to say, "Bless you," or when we meet someone on the street, we say, "Hello." But no one teaches us to show genuine interest in others, to have sincere interaction, or to show that we want to know more about them.

Fortunately, some people are naturally empathetic and look beyond what their eyes see. But not everyone has this value. Not everyone received this gift.

Just admit it, if someone asks, "How are you?" do you feel like they want to know how you are? Or is this another form of politeness, like saying "Hello"? Have you ever noticed that most people respond by saying, "Fine, thank you. And how are you?" All right, sure, let's not talk about the fact that most people are saying this while they're already walking away from you. And you are standing there thinking, *Are you kidding me?*

Now I realize that we can't jump to conclusions, as, in the end, everyone looks through their own set of glasses; they see through their background and their knowledge. You can't blame anyone for that.

They probably thought I was anti-social or wasn't interested in starting a conversation.
People don't have a crystal ball, and they make mistakes like every human does.

Now I'm more open to others. I'll take up the challenge and do my best to interact more with people. We'll see what happens. Are they finally going to see me?

Forced to fight.

"*It isn't about how hard you hit. It's about how hard you can get hit and keep moving forward. How much you can take and keep moving forward.*"

That is a well-known quote about resilience that is, without a doubt, known to all *Rocky* fans out there.

But when I look at myself today, my inner self is covered with bumps and bruises from all I had to go through on top of my daily battle with my body.

I didn't choose to fight, but I have to.
Nor did I choose to compete against a figurative Goliath, a.k.a. all things in life, as a little "nobody." I do it anyway.

How often have I heard "Give up and go on sick leave," and "It makes no sense why you do this to yourself," etc.?

Has it ever occurred to me to give up? No!

Why do I keep going on despite the hurt?
Because I know my worth and what I have to offer to my family and this world.

My body has been trying to stop me for years, and if I haven't allowed that, do you think I will break for Goliath?

Adversity tries to spit me out over and over again, and I experience pain each time, but I always get back up again, coming one step closer to my purpose.

Maybe not today or tomorrow, but the day will come when I stand on top of Goliath's shoulder and proudly look straight ahead at the rest of the world.

A fairy tale about Inclusion.

Once upon a time, there was a country where apples lived.

It was a beautiful land with fertile soil and gorgeous trees. They were the house of apples in which they grew. Until they were ripe to be picked up, each tree housed a kind of apple with its life purpose.

Every year, as soon as the apples were ripe and left their tree, the new apples came together in the village square. Each apple was allowed to express its purpose to be chosen by the invitees looking for them.

The village chief left all the newcomers in the middle of the circle, and the guests sat around it so they could observe each apple well to make their choice.

The head of the village picked an apple and asked, "What are you, a beautiful red/yellow apple? What do you have to offer?"

"I was born with an extra thin shell and am very crispy. No more work to do; you can eat me right away."

The head of the village went on to the next apple and asked, "What are you, a beautiful dark-red apple? What do you have to offer?"

Drops of Life Experience

"I was born with a raw shell, and I'm sweet and sour. You have to cook me, but you'll get a delicious apple chutney as a reward."

The guests seemed very interested, so the village head walked on and asked, "What are you, a beautiful yellow/green apple? What do you have to offer?"

"I was born with a red belly, and I'm aromatic. You have to press me, but as a reward, you'll get golden apple juice."

What a successful season; the guests were busy and looked very enthusiastic. However, the head of the village remained silent at an apple.

"Um, you're round like an apple, but you have a skin I can't describe, and your stem looks different. What do you bring to the table?"

"Yes, I am an apple, but I can't tell you why I was born. You can eat me raw or cooked or pressed."

The noise grew louder and louder. The chief of the village consulted with the guests and said,
"But you can't have different purposes in your life. You have to make a choice!"

"But I can't choose because my shell is thin, crispy, sweet, and aromatic. I can't change who I am. I am not the one who ought to make a choice; it's you."

The sequel to this story is up to you.

Politics.

This opinion stands loose from any political party.

I think politics is one of the few fields in the world where anyone can do anything.

I believe you ought to match the person with the most appropriate set of skills to a specific function—the concept of choosing the best person for the job.

Yet, in politics, a person is assigned a portfolio based on the number of votes their party received. And even this is not always the case if a politician makes alliances . . .

So, one time, a politician could be responsible for education, or for health care, for example; and the next time, they could be responsible for labor.

If you would do this at any company or organization, people would seriously doubt your mental abilities as a manager. But in this fourth dimension, it's all possible.

Hear ye, hear ye! The magical land of the magical unicorns does exist!

Unfortunately, it is completely disconnected from reality, where we ordinary mortals live.

Maybe I'm not a unicorn, but I'm probably the most loyal and reliable partner you could wish for.

Any form of sarcasm is coincidental.

THIS IS YOUR PERSONAL SPACE

Your journal

FEEL FREE TO WRITE WHATEVER YOU WANT

Open Mind: a metaphor.

Recently, an influencer posted an article about language errors, especially to use this as a reason to let go of a candidate in the race for a job. I watched in awe at how many reactions this article received, specifically how many mixed responses it got.

At home, the debate with my husband was tricky as well:

- I, who always worked as a customer service representative, noticed language errors but would not consider this a deal breaker.
- My husband, a warehouse coordinator, thinks the whole linguistic error debate is complete nonsense; and he gets angry at the thought of anyone being judged because of this. So, the topic is susceptible and touches on something that is ours.

How about a metaphor? I like metaphors to make a point.

Setting: the story takes place an Italian restaurant.
Situation: a couple goes to dinner.
First impression of the restaurant: it looked neat, with no fluff, but cared for.

Great, they are looking forward to what else it has to offer.

The couple opens the menu. Oh no! Language mistakes. She secretly looks toward the exit because, for a restaurant, your menu is your business card. If they ignored this, what else could have been overlooked? All kinds of "kitchen nightmare" scenarios wander through her head. Her partner isn't aware of this potential harm, does not notice the language errors, and is already dreaming of all the delicacies the chef has to offer. With so many choices there, he doesn't know what to choose.

She does not want to approach the evening negatively, so with great courage, she places an order despite the red flag. She has many doubts and fears as they wait for their dishes.

Hopefully, she didn't make a mistake by giving it a chance despite the warning . . .

But everything seems fine! The dishes look delicious and cared for, just like the first impression of the restaurant. No five-star presentation with a foam of this and a cloud of that; you see and know what you eat, and it's delicious!

What is the moral of the story?

People tend to jump to conclusions and make a mistaken judge of character. But plausible mistakes don't define a candidate or person. Give the candidate a fair opportunity to show what they stand for. Everyone deserves a chance.

Judge them based on their competencies, the abilities required for the job, and nothing else.

I was stunned.

I love getting up while everyone is still sleeping.
In a house where chaos and noise never come to rest, it's a delight to find a rare moment of peace.

In this fast-paced world we live in, when time is on your side, it's like the universe is throwing you a bone.

It's telling you to take this time and embrace it for what it truly is: a gift from what's beyond our comprehension.

Don't question it.
Don't let it slip away.
Please don't waste it.

Be content with what surrounds you.
Be content with what you have.
Be content with what is.

I believe in giving back.

I believe in giving back.

"If you can't help everyone, just help one." That is one of my credos; by "one," I am not referring to myself or others. Humans are not the only ones that might need help.

Adopting animals won't change the world, but it will change theirs forever.

I love animals and make it one of my life's purposes to help them whenever possible.

As a family, we have adopted nine pets over the years:

- two dogs
- two cats
- three guinea pigs
- two rabbits

And no, I'm not trying to rebuild Noah's Ark.

We are just committed to doing our part, too, to help.

Most of them were just abandoned, left on the street . . .

I can't grasp why anyone would do such a thing to a helpless being.

I am so grateful to those who rescue or adopt abandoned animals. But it's no joke, so please don't take this lightly, as it takes time, commitment, and money.

If you cannot care for them, please get in touch with the many animal shelters or associations that can take care of them and find them a home.

Just like us, animals deserve to be loved and taken care of.

In my humble opinion, how you treat animals says a lot about who you are as a human being.

If you are lucky enough to have an animal in your life, you can witness how loyal and loving they are.

They don't have great expectations.
They don't ask for much in return—just to be loved and cared for.
In return, you get a friend for life, a bond that lasts beyond.

The absurdity of it all.

Some of you might have heard of some people's actions to adapt classic novels.

But why would anyone try to change the past?

It's not by denial that it didn't take place.
It's not by hiding its evidence that it won't reoccur.

A book ban or rewriting classic novels or history books is not only disrespecting the author's work, but it also increases the chances of making the same mistakes, which ironically is the exact opposite of its intent.

So let the past be.

Find your peace with it.

Don't get blindsided by someone's attempt to keep your mind from what matters.
Understand the real issues and shift your focus to what you can do to bring significant change.

As it's our present and future, we need to worry about it.

Life finds a way.

That is one of my favorite quotes because of its simplicity, insight, and truth.
Take these beautiful raspberries, for instance.

Believe it or not, they come straight out of our garden.

And I might be gifted with some things, but gardening isn't one of them.
Even cactuses won't last in my home.

We planted one branch of a raspberry plant just a little over a year ago.

I didn't know if it needed care.
Nor did I know if it was in the right place.
I didn't know if it was the right season.

Mmm, I just love raspberries; I bought the branch and planted it.

Some folks with gardening experience in my family thought I was wild, thinking this wouldn't work out. The plant would be dead in no time.

And as you can see, even if I didn't care for it, even if I didn't prepare for it, and even if I didn't follow instructions, the plant grew just fine, and these are the results.

Because life finds a way.

And it's the same for other matters in life. As long as you believe it will and believe in what you do and what you want, life will take its course and bring results in time.

You can follow all the instructions to the letter, even use tactics and strategy, yet that approach still doesn't mean guaranteed success.

Some things will work out just fine without any preparation, as long as you have positive thoughts and simple faith and confidence in what you're doing.

Life finds a way.

Anticipation is the best part.

This is it!
It's make-or-break time.

I'm ready to put my words down on paper.

Last night I couldn't fall asleep (so typical), as my mind was set, and my mind overloaded.

As I tried to fall asleep my mind kept working on my book in my mind for the entire night.

As soon as I woke up one morning, I went on my Canva profile.

I bet you thought I went straight to writing.
Well, no, I'm sure fellow writers will get it.

So, I went to Canva to make two book covers:
- ✔ soft, elegant Japanese style
- ✔ fierce, modern design style

I have been staring at them, attempting to make my choice. Being a Scorpio, I'm decisive, yet they are so different. People buy first with their eyes.

Okay, okay, I'm letting it rest for now.

And I would start writing the same day!

I always appreciate the support and advice from my audience.

What an exciting moment. I always tell my kids, "Anticipation is the best part!"

Self-care.

"If you can't help everyone, just help one."
This is one of my favorite credos, as helping others is my core talent. I wish to inspire and, hopefully, help others.

However, the first person you need to help is yourself, and if you don't take care of yourself, you'll never be able to be there for anyone else.

Learn to take care of your body, as that is your home, and you wouldn't leave your household uncared for, right?

Over the years, I've made some life-changing decisions that I'm proud of:
- ✓ I don't drink soda anymore.
- ✓ I don't eat red meat anymore.
- ✓ I don't drink alcohol anymore.
- ✓ I do a 20-minute daily workout.

Self-discipline will bring you much further than motivation ever will.

Motivation will ignite your energy, yet self-discipline will keep the fire burning over time.

THIS IS YOUR PERSONAL SPACE

Your journal

FEEL FREE TO WRITE WHATEVER YOU WANT

DROP THREE:

POEMS OF LIFE

I never saw myself as capable
Of writing poetry. I believe it to be
Such a refined art, and I am
Anything but refined.
Yet, thanks to a writing prompt,
Where you had to write
A poem around one word,
I took the challenge and started writing.
I liked it, as it's an abstract, artistic
Way of talking about severe aspects of life.
It has a genuine yet mysterious side,
Which allows me to share even those things
I'm not ready to talk about.

Rebellion

I was done going to what
was supposed to be my
safe heaven, fearing
for the person who
was meant to take
good care of me
forever.

I could not bear another
minute of this ache.

The time had come
for
rebellion.

Resilient

Life's adversities offer you
opportunity in disguise.

The opportunity to show
your inner strength.

The kind of strength you
didn't even know you had.

Once you are forced to
use that inner strength,
you'll know what it
means to be
resilient.

Atrocity

Taking someone's life in the name of honor.

Taking your own child's life to cleanse

your family name.

No regret.

No judgment.

No resentment.

Yet it's a pure

atrocity.

Human by Nature

What a wonderful event it is to witness year after year,

how nature comes alive.

Just like my white roses,

I'm woken up by early summer's warmth.

Revived by its promise.

I blossom and reveal myself as I am.

Beautiful and flawed.

Human by Nature

Punk

I love music.

More than words, it can transfer

emotions in just one instant.

Without saying anything,

its flow,

its rhythm.

Music

is dynamic

it creates

a feeling,

a mood, a vibe.

Witness the masters at work.

Put on some Daft Punk.

Child

I got emotional while I listened to my younger self.

I felt a deep sense of sympathy,

a deep sense of solitude,

and a deep sense of sorrow.

I wanted to reach out,

hug me.

That hug I was

aching for as

a child.

Damaged

A fallen plane, broken.

A wrecked bike, broken.

A shattered glass, broken.

A cluttered mind, damaged.

A wounded soul, damaged.

A broken heart, damaged.

Things when broken,

are thrown away.

Useless.

People, when damaged,

are healed in time.

Stronger.

Personality

Who am I?

Who are you?

What differentiates us from each other?

You're a person

and I am too.

How would I be any different

from you?

Personality, she says.

That's what makes me, me.

That's what makes you, you.

At Dawn

As the day is ending,

I am off to rest,

as my mind needs to

reboot.

At dawn,

that is.

Fate

I believe fate
brought us together.
I was unaware of
my future.
Yet fate knew and brought
me to you,
so you could help me
get through.
Fate knew I needed to be
loved by
you.
My forever friend.
My guardian angel.

Feminist

Life was given by a woman

through birth.

Love was given by a woman

through care.

Laughter was given by a woman

through joy.

Women,

be proud,

be genuine,

be confident,

be feminist,

as you truly are

life's essence.

For without you,

there is none.

Radiate

Always take care of the ones

dear to you.

Their love will radiate

upon your soul.

Termite

When we were together,

I felt consumed,

eaten from

within.

His toxic narcissism

was destroying my

mind.

I was losing my

inner self.

Just like a termite

eats its way

through

wood,

he

was

eating

his way

through me.

Healing

Sharing is

the first

step

toward

Healing.

Let it all out,

or it will

weigh

you

D

O

W

N

Haunting

Even after
all
these years,
you still
keep
haunting
me.
I can still
smell your skin,
hear your voice,
feel your touch.

I dread
every
part
of it.

When
Will I
be freed
from
you?

19:34

My father passed away

three years ago.

He was born in 1934,

and for years now,

as I watch

the clock,

I look at the exact moment

when it is

19:34.

Coincidence?

Sign?

Inclusive Employer

Where are you,

inclusive employer?

I've been looking for you.

Every day, I see

interesting messages

as my fear of drowning increases.

Again and again,

I give myself courage,

but it takes

oh so long

for my new beginning.

Why don't they see me?

Why do I see comments passing me by?

Oh, where are you,

my new start?

I long for you with all my heart.

Will I get another chance

to do my bit?

Will there be a viable job after all this time?

What would I like to be,

helpful to others,

show who I am,

and throw my skills into the fight.

Despite everything,

I keep hoping.

I keep dreaming

that, one day,

we will meet.

Sunset

And, as the earth

is yet

making

another turn,

the sun sets

upon

my day.

Trying

Seeing kindness,

generosity toward

someone who's

trying to

live their

dream.

To be able to share a passion

for writing and being apt to

motivate and inspire

others.

Word by word,

step by step,

I'll get there.

Curiosity

Curiosity is

what keeps

the mind young.

To be apt to look at

the world

through the eyes

of a learner.

To see everyday things,

eager to understand

more about them.

I'm curious by nature,

and I hope never

to lose that

feature.

It provides endless

inspiration.

Kindness

To be kind means
to be apt to see
who's in front
of you,

as there cannot
be kindness if
there's no
Knowledge.

It begins by
acknowledging
who you are
and what you went through.

A smile, a nod, a wink,
that's all it takes
to begin an act
of kindness.

Wisdom

Wisdom is the reward
for the lessons
we've learned.
All the things we felt were
mistakes gave us
something in return.

A gift to
our soul,
our mind.

Don't be blind to it.
Grasp it and be
thankful for it.
It will help us,
maybe not
today.
But
someday
it will.

New Year's Reflection

The end of 2022 is approaching,

and my desire for

a new start remains

unchanged.

While others celebrate and rejoice,

I keep watching and searching,

and I can't enjoy myself

as most.

The inevitable ticking clock

worries me.

I would love to let go

and

not keep counting

until tomorrow.

The holiday season is always

Drops of life experience

a very stressful period,

especially now

that I post everything online

in an inescapable manner.

Being highly sensitive is now

twice as hard.

The hopeless situation around work

makes it oh so difficult.

I do my best for my husband and children.

Hopefully,

my worries will diminish

soon.

Helping others

is very important to me.

May the new year 2023
offer me

opportunities

so I can achieve my goal and contribute.

THIS IS YOUR PERSONAL SPACE

Your journal

FEEL FREE TO WRITE WHATEVER YOU WANT

Perseverance

Focus and perseverance are key.

Keep your objective in sight.

Reflect, observe, and make a plan.

When the time comes, be ready to

put your plan into action.

Be patient, as outstanding achievements

take time to build.

Move as slowly as you need,

as long as you keep moving forward.

There will be ups and downs,

not to worry, as long as you keep moving.

It doesn't matter

how many times you fall,

as long as you don't

stay down.

Get up and try again,

for as long as you

need to get

where you want

to be.

A Pun

A wedding to

be

celebrated.

A younger

sister

versus her

elder.

She thanks

all who

offended

the bride.

That's not

what

the text read.

She made

a pun

in front of

the entire

church.

Yet no one laughed.

Her mistaken wish

came true.

Escape

Alone facing

evil.

Stuck.

No way out

when your worst

nightmare is called

H

O

M

E

No emergency exits.

A child with

nowhere

to go to,

except for

her

imagination.

Her only

escape.

Her true

savior.

Make Time

You make time

for the things

that matter

to you.

For time

is the most

wonderful gift

you have to give.

The Day Begins.

As the day begins,

new hope is found.

Hope for a better day.

Hope for a better feeling.

Hope for a better outcome.

Whatever your hope for

this new day might be,

I wish you

the best

only.

The Sky

The sky is shifting

colors,

just like a snake

does to its

skin.

We get rid of

the old,

wait for the

new.

Tomorrow's sky

will be

different

and so will

you.

Be the Best Version

I often read posts,

encouraging

people to be

the best at

what they do.

I don't aim to be "the best."

Why should anyone?

It's a recipe for

disaster.

Being the *best* version of

yourself,

that's what you should

aim for.

Technology

Growing up in a world
without
smartphones or social media
technology often seems like
a curse.
Touch screens
drive me mad.
How I long for the days when
there was face-to-face human
interaction without buffering.
To speak to someone,
you had to make an effort,
call them on the phone, or go
to their house. If you wanted to
leave a message, you took a
pen and paper and wrote
down your words.

No way to hide behind a screen
in your "cocoon." It showed
character; it showed interest.
It's ironic, as now we are only
a click away but
miles apart.

Trust

Imagine a nice hot bath,

enjoying the warmth of every

drop of water, which is

embracing you tenderly

while you're playing

with the scented soap bubbles.

You feel safe; you feel surrounded

by love and affection.

This is my metaphor for a happy life,

free of troubles or worries.

The water is your environment.

The bubbles are the people in your life.

Imagine removing the plug

from the bathtub; all the water is irrevocably

drained, and you watch it flow away fast, however

powerless to stop it. Your

safe and loving environment changed into a deserted

and empty place in just a few moments.
Only a few soap bubbles are still sticking
to the tub.

This is what happens when things go wrong
when you're going through hard times.

People show their true colors, as
It's easy being there for you when
everything goes well; however, when
things go wrong. Only a few remain to support
you. It's in those moments in life that you realize
who you can trust, who you can rely on.

Please don't waste your time and energy on those who aren't there
when you need them the most. Embrace the ones who
stick with you, just like those soap bubbles in the tub.

Community

A sense of belonging.

A sense of family.

A sense of home.

How long have I

searched

for you?

I looked everywhere,

at work,

at school.

Nothing.

Until I joined

the writing

community.

I was always looking

in the real world,

yet I found you

online.

A Moment to Remember

As the sun sets upon a part of my life,

I look behind me and see

all the struggles I went through.

Though I am grateful for the changes I made,

the lessons learned, and the people I've met,

I look at my kids and see the hope in their eyes,

the promise of a new beginning, love, and pride.

My husband looks excited but anxious

about what the next months might bring.

He still has confidence in me.

As the sun sets upon a part of my life,

I look ahead and see

my professional dream come true,

my future within reach,

and my evolution in life.

Premature

Excruciating
pain,
leaving your
firstborn infant
behind.

All alone in the
neonatal care unit
with other
premature
babies.

How I wept.
How I cursed.
How I worried
for you, my child.

The hardest thing
I've ever had to do,
by far.

But we're together
now.

Ballerina

Have you ever
looked at the stars
above?
Sparkling bright dots,
connecting
the universe.
Imagine what
it would be like
being able to
jump from
one star
to the other.
Like a ballerina
dancing,
twirling
in the
night sky.

Breathe

When you don't know

what to do,

what to say,

what to write,

take time,

stand still,

and

just

breathe.

Between

An inner battle

trying to

balance

between

being a mom

and

being a

woman,

as, from birth,

both are

forever

entwined.

An unbreakable

bond

between

mother and child.

Yet the woman

within

Drops of Life Experience

longs for

me-time.

No guilt.

No judgment,

for you're

only

human.

Maybe

Why is it that

we can't keep

our options open?

Why do we have

to choose right away?

Sometimes, you

take

a moment

to reflect,

to decide,

to contemplate.

Sometimes, we

can't just

say yes

or

say no.

Drops of life experience

Sometimes, it's

not obvious.

Sometimes, all

we know is

maybe.

THIS IS YOUR PERSONAL SPACE

Your journal

FEEL FREE TO WRITE WHATEVER YOU WANT

DROP FOUR:

THOUGHTS ON LIFE

These are little reminders,

little quotes or

some excerpts from the book,

to help you keep your mindset boosted.

Perhaps

You could read one a day

while having your morning coffee

or read whenever you feel low

and need a little help

from a friend.

You chose

how you read these;

my thoughts are here

for you

whenever you need them.

It's like a tennis match; the set goes to one kid one time and the next to the other. Please don't feel guilty; we all have favorites occasionally. As long as it's balanced between the kids, I think it's okay and very human.

No apology is needed—you have the right to say no, and you ought to when you feel you've reached the limit. And don't put pressure on yourself; do one thing at a time—brick by brick, task by task, design by design, just manageable steps. You can do it.

Just take your pictures as I do. You can't be more authentic and original.

Let me put it this way: if I'm constantly thinking about my emails, I won't be able to enjoy my vacation anyway, so it's better and healthier for me to check them; and the ache will go away. It's a choice you must make for yourself; ask yourself what will benefit you the most.

People expect the truth from us. If you don't know something, always say, "I don't know, but I'll find out for you." Reassurance is essential to set up a lasting relationship based on trust.

◊

Self-care should be about your mind and health—inner care—though most people only care for their surface, but that's beauty care. The balance should be the other way around. Well, I'm finally working on my book, which is inner care for me, as I can now stop thinking about it and do it.

◊

It sounds simple, yet letting go is one of the hardest lessons I've learned. It took me almost burning out to realize why I needed to know to do it ASAP. And in time, I did. I learned to let go of the time- and energy-consuming things I couldn't change. And yes, it makes life a lot lighter. Get rid of the clutter in your mind.

◊

I have never been a sheep that follows the herd and never will be. So, propaganda doesn't work. I have always followed my path, and I always will.

◊

I always tell my kids to cheer for someone, never against them. That's my way of making them positive. The energy you put out there will resonate back on you.

It's like adding a bit of Fleur de Sel to your dish, which will lift its taste. However, if the other ingredients aren't flavorful, the salt won't help it.

◊

My family comes first. Always. They are my main reason for everything I do, as everything I do is for them.

◊

Sometimes, pretending is the only way you have to survive. I did it too. My "fake" self got me through my childhood. Now I'm free to be myself. What you see or read is what you get. If you don't like it, keep scrolling.

◊

I'm a mom, so giving to others without expecting anything in return is all I do.

◊

I've always been an advocate for on-the-job learning. All you need is a bit of goodwill and a large spoon of eagerness to learn to grow. You can do many things if you combine that type of learning with the basic skills you already have. Just go for it and see where it might bring you. And remind yourself you can always go back with gained experience.

◊

We need to find our balance; that's the key to a healthy mind: balance—no more, no less.

Like many things in life, I had to make mistakes and gain knowledge and awareness to get where I am now, at forty-one. Life means change, and change means evolving.

Oh yeah, inspiration can hit you at any given time or place. Be prepared to keep track. You can use a little notepad like the one Columbo used to have, where he penciled down everything while he interviewed his suspects. It doesn't take up much space, and you'll be happy you'll take it with you.

It's ironic how, in freelance, having different kind of jobs for short periods of time in your career is called pivoting, and everybody can see why this is of great value to gain experience. Still, in the regular employee role, this is considered an inconsistent career path, meaning that you are not serious about it or that employers don't want to take you on board. I'm so happy I'm done with that sh*t and am part of the "free world" now.

Finding the right words does matter, especially in delicate or tense situations.

This is exactly how I studied for my exams, copying essential parts. In the end, I ended up with my version of the syllabus, which was printed in my mind through writing.

Don't let the negativity of others turn off your light. Don't be afraid to shine.

I'm just telling it as it is, no hacks, shortcuts, or easy way out. Just take your time and build your business one brick at a time. The outcome will be more rewarding.

I always tell my kids that anticipation is the best part. At first, they didn't understand, as they just wanted the big day (Christmas, birthday . . .) to arrive ASAP. But now the eldest gets it, and every year when a big day for him comes, he tells me, "Mom, you're right; anticipation is the best part."

Society kept spitting me back out because of my disability. So, I cut all the strings loose and liberated myself by becoming a solopreneur. I took back control over my life, and now I'm in charge of the steering wheel, choosing which direction to turn. And I don't regret it one bit.

I'm highly sensitive and introverted, so I mainly kept to myself as long as possible, opening up only to some. I don't trust easily. It's all uphill from there when you can't trust the person who put you on this earth. And yes, I am a survivor, living in survival mode most of my life. It wasn't until I became a mom myself, when I finally found out what motherhood was, that I learned what unconditional love was. I'm so grateful for all I have.

⬦

Always make your reader see the big picture. Writing per se has no meaning for people, except for the one that writes. Therefore, what you write and the effect it will have on people matters so much. Think wisely about your choice of words.

⬦

I feel so old now . . . but that's so typical of me. Nothing came easy to me, I didn't have anything the simple or the fast way. Fighting, always, harder than anybody I knew. Yet I am confident that I'll get there. You will see me struggle, but you'll never see me quit—mic drop.

⬦

I have many things to be proud of. I am a mom of two kids, ten and eleven years old, and my husband is with me. It's hard for the two of us to deal with everything, so I can only applaud single mothers like you for doing all the work. I'm a survivor, too, and it brought everything back to the surface when I became a mom. So, I got help from a counselor, as I knew I couldn't get through it alone. And it helped me chase my demons away. It is a lifetime recovery.

◊

It's absurd to think that anything we do to earn a living, even if it is a side business, will be a walk in the park. We still have to put in the work: project - plan - invest time/effort. Money doesn't fall from the sky, no matter how little it might be.

◊

It makes total sense. We should be more grateful for what we have and the chances we get to take. Life can be such a lottery, as where you're from (in the world or society) dictates how your life will be. If you're on LinkedIn, chances are you're one of the ones. Free to create opportunities.

◊

My main focus is to inspire and motivate people by sharing genuine stories of events.

◊

Our body wasn't conceived to stay still; it was made to be on the move. This is a simple truth you should tell yourself every day; it will motivate you to get up and move. No fitness needed, but get up and move.

It's always easier in retrospect to criticize what you did. I've been there too; I was a workaholic, eager to take on more and more. Also, I was kind of proud of it . . . I almost burned out years ago. One of the first things I had to learn was "to say no," which was tough. As I'm happy to help, it still is challenging to say no, but we all have to draw the line at some point. Find your balance.

◊

My inspiration can come from just about anything. I'm an eager learner and am interested in a large variety of topics. I like LinkedIn; there's so much to learn and interesting people to engage with. It's like a catered event. Take your pick.

◊

If you master letting go, your life will greatly benefit. It will be a lot lighter.

◊

The bond you share with an animal lasts a lifetime. They have a pure way of touching your soul; they can communicate without words. I'm a sucker for ??. We have adopted nine animals over the years (not to speak of those who have already left us), and I have to refrain myself, as I can't stand the idea of an abandoned animal. How you treat them says a lot about who you are as a human being.

◊

DROPS OF LIFE EXPERIENCE

I'm a survivor too. *The Bold and the Beautiful* plots are peanuts compared to my life. But I always got back up and kept going forward because I believed there was more to life. I don't know if it's a coincidence, as I just wrote about one of those plots today. If you have time, have a look. Let's support each other.

◊

People expect the truth; they will see right through you if you're fake. Asking for help is a sign of great strength and courage, as owning up to your issues and deciding to face them isn't easy.

◊

It never stopped raining, yet I have an umbrella now.

◊

I'm a nerd, so I like doing things for myself, on my terms, and deciding what is a priority and what's not. That's the whole deal; nobody tells me what to do and when. I'm free to handle what I enjoy doing as I see fit, and that's freedom to me.

◊

Having an online community, that's my goal. Sharing thoughts, learning from each other, inspiring one another. That's the intention.

It's not easy exposing yourself, yet I wanted others to see that you can overcome whatever the challenge ahead may be. Have faith in yourself, no matter what. You're worth it.

◊

That's why I shared my experience, so others could see what I learned: where there's a willingness to go forward despite the challenges it holds, there's a way.

◊

It's all about perception. We all see things through our glasses, so for some, an issue can be huge, yet the same problem seems worthless of attention to others. The feeling is subjective, so there is no judgment whatsoever. Know that reaching out and talking about it might help you see things differently.

◊

When you start losing sleep over it, all that extra energy going through your body caused by your excitement, that's when you know you're on the right track. You can always catch up on your sleep later.

◊

It's your self-preservation. After almost burning out years ago, one of the first lessons I learned was to say no more often. I was always the first to help others, yet I forgot to care for myself. And if you don't take care of yourself, nobody else will. It's not selfish to put yourself first; if you don't care for yourself, you won't be able to care for others.

Drops of Life Experience

◊

It seems so noble to want to help others in distress. However, it should be standard for all of us. One of my credos is, "If you can't help everyone, just help one." Because if we all did this, nobody would be left alone in this world.

◊

Loyalty is a great virtue, and it's so rare these days, as people are so inconsistent. Unreliable even.

◊

All starts with you, and you need to build a foundation first. Your foundation is to take care of yourself. That's how you'll create a solid and resistant foundation. Only when you achieve that can you begin to build the next level, and the next one, and the next one. If your foundation is strong, there's no limit on how high you can build on top of it.

◊

It wasn't easy at first, as I was afraid to reproduce the same behavior I received as a kid because that was the only way I knew. So, I went to counseling for help, which was good. It helped me see that I was different from the one who raised me and that I could give my kids the love and affection I never received. Even hugs and kisses were hard in the beginning. Can you imagine? Now they are ten and eleven, and hugs and kisses are the most natural thing.

◊

The beauty of it is that you can easily take a little break by leaving your mobile device in another room for a while, so you won't get tempted to take it and have a look; and you won't hear the notifications. When you're ready to get back to it, you do. That's my way of unplugging a few times a day, even for half an hour. But it does feel good to be just me for a while.

Work isn't personal; it's a means to an end. Yet my work is very personal as a self-employed solopreneur. I am what I do. I am my work.

Building a business isn't just about the company but about you and your dream. While you're working hard on it, you're working hard on yourself. Brick by brick, you're building yourself.

Since they were little, I have taught my kids to read every day. Whether they like it or not, they read two pages a day, as it enhances their level of understanding. And that's important if you want to learn.

I'm a big fan of *Rocky*; it still inspires me every time I watch it. I, too, launched myself at forty-one for the same reason, knowing that I couldn't live with myself if I kept denying the essence of being a writer. I also turned down government financial aid to be completely free of burden. It's my responsibility to make it work with the little I have, but I, too, have learned how to manage on a small amount of income; and I don't need much to be content. It's all about mindset.

◊

I'm against hacks in every form. Just do the work, make an effort, and you'll feel even more proud when the results come. At least I do.

◊

My photography is mostly about nature, family, and animals. I like to capture the moment with no planning or posing. Sometimes, my inspiration begins with the picture, and I add the text after; other times, it's the opposite. On Instagram, I also add music when it adds to the emotion I feel and wish to transmit to my reader.

◊

To avoid eating at night, brushing my teeth right after dinner will do the trick, as I'm too lazy to do it again later.

◊

I'm a forever learner, and that's why I like platforms such as LinkedIn, as you keep learning new things on a daily basis and meeting interesting and resourceful people along the way; and I try to do my part. It's been a challenging yet fulfilling journey.

I know I always treat others like I would want to be treated by them. So, I am respectful and kind. Of course, I am human, thus flawed, so when I have a terrible day, it might show through it all. But from what I have experienced, human "sharks" tend to be harsher on kind people, as they feel you won't bite back. At least not at once, and they take advantage. So kind, yes; naive, no.

◊

It's like the "after" experts who give their immaculate advice on how we should have handled something that has already happened (the pandemic, for instance). That's such a comfy place to talk from, as you can't say anything wrong; the knowledge is already there . . . Just write new books with today's insights, as there is always something to learn. Let the past be. It's done.

◊

Indeed, time is one of the most valuable things in life, and we never know when we will run out of it or when adversity will hit and put all our plans on hold. I know firsthand . . . So, use it for the things that matter, make choices, and don't forget to make time for yourself.

◊

A leader is actively involved with their team, motivating and guiding them.

As long as I feel good, I couldn't care less if someone thinks I'm not cool enough. I believe that feeling good about what you do and what you represent is the most important thing.

Oh yeah, as soon as money is involved, all bells go off. Be aware of scammers.

It is so important to take time for ourselves and declutter our minds, or at least try to have a moment of pure relaxation. Sometimes, you need a reminder.

Rules are made to keep us from complete chaos and anarchy. Some practices are also made to be altruistic. For instance, if you are the type of person who would park in a parking spot reserved for people with disabilities just to be somewhere earlier, I can't see tolerating that, as you are creating a problem for someone who needs the spot. And if you are running late, you should have left earlier or taken public transportation. The same goes for speeding. You need to be prepared and take responsibility for your actions. Whenever you want to break a rule, think, *Will I harm someone by doing this?* If the answer is, *Yes, I might*, just don't do it. I am a mom, so I take these things seriously, as I need to raise two boys with healthy values.

To give back to those in need means the world. It's something to be proud of.

◊

In the end, you can only do your best and keep doing it as long as possible—or as long as you are motivated. Remember why you started in the first place and then remind yourself of that initial sentiment and drive. Those will lift you when your motivation is at its lowest. It's all about mindset.

◊

I couldn't fit in, even if I tried. I have been the odd duck forever. Only when I was thirty-five and did some career coaching did my coach explain what being a highly sensitive person meant. Suddenly, a lightbulb lit in my mind, as I fully recognized myself in the description. Yet the fact remains that I'm different, and that's a good thing.

◊

Life doesn't come with an instruction manual, so how could someone ever claim to be apt to coach you in life? Are we playing a game? Soccer, maybe? Your life is not a game. It is your endgame. However, you can guide people the best you can.

◊

I learned the hard way that health is priceless; without it, your entire life comes to a standstill. Everyone ought to make their health the number one priority in their life. Minor adjustments in daily life can be powerful tools to increase and protect your health. Yet again, it's all about mindset.

◊

Be proud of yourself and take it easy, as healing will be a long-term process of temptation, denial, motivation, willingness, etc. It's emotional, and you can only do your best.

◊

I wouldn't define myself as being a pro or an expert at anything, yet I am experienced and have knowledge to share. And that's precisely what I do on LinkedIn and other platforms; if I can help even one person, that is the whole purpose.

◊

My father passed away just three years ago, and I would have done more to help him if I had known about his condition. But I didn't know about it. It came so quickly, during the pandemic, but after things were opening up again after the first lockdown. I got a call, rushed to the hospital, and saw a man I hardly recognized. He couldn't speak. The very next day, he was gone. Cherish the moments you have together; afterward, those memories will mean the world to you.

◊

I have always felt for students who have to borrow money to be able to study and hope for a better future. I studied for six years after high school and didn't have to borrow money. But I was lucky to have been born and live in Western Europe. So sad and unfair that where we are born influences our lives and futures in such a powerful way. Life shouldn't be a lottery.

○

It's about time we join the two ends of the same chain instead of separating them with a cold "seller/buyer" term. There is no hierarchy here, only collaboration.

○

I went six months without social media after my father passed away three years ago. I just needed to unplug and focus on myself and my family. I didn't miss it until, one day, I felt curious enough to open it up again, so I did. But it's good to know I could live without it. It's even reassuring.

○

My integrity can't be bought, not now, not ever.

○

I never believed in copy/paste solutions. Just look at love advice, medical treatments, or even cooking recipes. You'll end up having different procedures and outcomes. Why? First, as humans, we are all equal yet different in character and at heart. Second, there are variables, some of which we can't control—some of which we can't even explain. So yes, experiment and find what works for you. If you set your heart to it, be patient, keep going, and watch as the magic happens.

DROPS OF LIFE EXPERIENCE

◊

We are all on a learning path, no matter which side we are on, the information provider or the recipient. Along the way, we will assess and adjust, get new intel, provide it to the audience, and repeat.

◊

Just be honest, which the reader expects. If you are fake, they'll see right through you.

◊

It's not easy to see your body change as a woman, after childbirth and as you grow older. As we are not oblivious and have mirrors, there is no need to be reminded of every little detail confirming what we already know has changed. It's so harmful and unnecessary. What matters is your health and how you feel. Positive words from the outside can help us embrace our body through its changes. But it always starts with a mindset. If you learn to love yourself as you are, you've already won.

◊

Since I had kids, I have lost all sense of time. It happens so often that I reply to a message only to realize afterward that I had only answered it in my head . . .

◊

Choices make our lives for ourselves, and our vision and values make those decisions. Through the choices we make, the words we say, and the actions we take, we show our true colors. Our clients, friends, and coworkers will like us more or less for it. That's fundamental human nature, and that's okay, as they, too, have to decide if they want to work with us, make friends with us, or do business with us. Show yourself, and the "right" match will come your way and vice versa.

○

I hate comparisons so much, and so many variables make it quite impossible to compare one person to another. Whenever I hear my kids compare themselves to others, I get outraged. Why put yourself in such a position only to diminish yourself? Humans like to self-destruct when things don't go our way, and it starts so young. What a pity.

○

After my car accident back in '09, I was covered in bruises, and while sedated in the ICU, I heard the staff refer to me as Smurf (you know, from the cartoons?) But I recovered after months of physical therapy (still ongoing), and I am trying to make the most of it despite the chronic pain. So, I humbly believe I am pretty resilient.

○

Well, when you find yourself in such a situation, either you fight or don't. I chose to fight.

DROPS OF LIFE EXPERIENCE

No matter what you do for a living, be proud as you take responsibility for yourself and your family. You are making an honest life for yourself and contributing to society, which is respectful and honorable.

Every time I see someone online bragging about a certain amount of money, being rich, and such, I scroll the hell out of there. I'm on a different mindset, earning a good living doing what I love (which is priceless); however, we can all enjoy life and make dreams happen, whatever they may be.

Not being paid is awful; however, someone ghosting you on top of everything is even worse. You feel disrespected as a professional and dismissed as a person. That hurts on a personal level.

I am a mom, too, and often see intolerance toward kids. Newsflash! They don't come with a remote; we can't press a mute button. Yet they are part of life; like everything surrounding us (traffic, electronics, people), they aren't silent. Just be tolerant.

I don't believe in quitting. However, there is a nuance between quitting in the sense of stopping and doing nothing and leaving to do something else. The latter is redirecting, and that is a smart move. Only you know what's best for you, for your career. Take a moment and take some distance to see things more clearly. The answer will come to you.

◊

I want to help others through my own stories of life. If I can inspire, or educate even, that will be amazing. Positively touching the lives of others is such an honor.

◊

I've been a chronic overthinker most of my life; that mindset consumes time and energy and causes extra stress and anxiety. Since I turned thirty-five, I have been learning the art of letting go, and things have improved. I'm not done with it, but it is a game-changer.

◊

Have a plan and be prepared; that is the best way to cope with life's expected and unexpected events. It makes you confident, and it keeps you calm and less anxious.

◊

Evolution takes time, just as all fundamental changes do. Transition is a part of life; we all go through it at one point or another. You see, learn new information, and evolve. The basic skill of survival is essential to any form of life.

Drops of Life Experience

💧

Don't be too hard on yourself; try to handle one thing at a time. It's hard seeing a loved one fade away right in front of you. You feel helpless, useless, numb... but we are all human beings just trying to get through the day. So are you.

💧

Negative people tend to drag you down in negativism, but positive people will lift you with optimism. Choose your company with good sense, as people around you have a lot more impact on your life than you realize.

💧

I promote curiosity in my kids. I have always been curious, questioning everything and wanting to know and understand things. Today, at forty-one, I am still like that. With Google search and such, today's kids have so many easy and quick tools in their hands, making their curiosity and longing for research low. We need to do something to motivate them, to develop that part of them. How? For instance, I have a subscription to *National Geographic Junior* magazines for my kids to encourage them to search things out for themselves; and I send them to play outside. Let's do our part as parents.

💧

Moms are underrated; that is why I refer to myself as "Mama Manager." Running a household is like running a business, without vacation time and no pay. How about a round of applause for all working moms out there? You are amazing!

When you ask for someone's opinion, you'll get someone's opinion. Put it into perspective and leave it to rest. Once you're ready to look at your work through the eyes of others, you'll see if their opinions have some truth in them or not. It stays the receiver's decision in the end.

It's true that negative feelings are such a burden to the person carrying them. Mastering the art of letting go and forgiving others means setting yourself free and making your life lighter.

I have learned (with age) to let go of things I can't control to not put energy into them, as it would be a waste. I would have known valuable lessons earlier, as they make your life relatively easier!

When you take a step back, you see the greater picture.

Timing is an essential variable in life, and it can make or break any situation. Just be patient.

When I share my personal stories, I hope to touch people's lives and maybe help them in their relatable struggles. Even if only one person reads it, as long as I've been helpful, I will have succeeded in my task.

◊

I, too, am a child of immigration. Is it a coincidence that we share the same values and views? I don't believe it is. Embrace your roots, cherish the values given to you, and lay them upon the new generations.

◊

I apply caution while posting or talking with people online, as you never know who is on the other end. I teach the same insights to my kids (ten and eleven) as they game online. We need to keep ourselves and our loved ones safe from any potential harm. Thank you for talking about this aspect of us being online.

◊

I am an instinctive writer and put the words down when inspiration comes. I wouldn't say I like to plan a posting time. If it goes well, that's great. If the algorithm sends me to oblivion, that's too bad, but yet again, I will have learned something from it.

◊

Yes, drop the clutter of all needless words. You must look at every word in a sentence and ask yourself, *Is this word doing something? Is it telling something on its own?* If the answer is no, remove it. All words you use need to tell, or they are out.

◊

I don't know why you would treat someone like crap just because they are doing their job. All parts of society meet on LinkedIn and other social platforms for that matter. We all have our reason to be there. Treat each other with respect, just as you would in real life. Good old courtesy goes a long way.

◊

I had to use some good moves to overcome my turbulent journey. Now, I'm riding steadily on a high wave.

◊

If you can't adopt, you can foster sick animals until they get better. You can volunteer at a shelter or donate food/blankets/etc. They can all use help; they are such wonderful people.

◊

Always stay in motion, keep moving, and be open to the new information you'll gain. It's a learning process that takes time.

◊

It's like giving someone a testimonial. I think it's a pity we should ask for them on LinkedIn or any other site. It would be more sincere and meaningful if the person gave the testimonial without being asked. That would genuinely show what they think of you.

It's a huge responsibility, as we can influence other people's lives with our words, even if that's not our intention. It's a great privilege to touch people's lives and help them on their journeys. The two are very much linked to each other. It's our responsibility to choose the right words, think about how we say them, and express our purpose.

The maze is the grandpa of today's escape rooms. It's ironic how people will pay to get lost and find the way out, even though most are lost but aren't doing anything about it. The thrill of making it out, of finding the solution, is exciting. And if you can't find it on your own, reach out for help. No sign of weakness. It's just common sense. The purpose is to find your way out; nobody said you should do it alone.

What about beginner's luck? You've never done it before so that no preparation could have helped you. Many unexplainable things in life beat the odds. It's like karma, believing it will return if you send positivity into the universe. It's the same with negativity.

But you can wish for luck, which is just as powerful because you have an open mindset for positive things to happen. It's like I was telling my son the other day while he was stressing about a test at school. I told him, if he goes to school thinking he won't do well, the chances are far more significant that he will fail. If he goes with a winner's mindset, telling himself he will crush it, chances are he will—a self-fulfilling prophecy.

Since I was a child I have always loved questioning. I am a critical thinker, so it's nonstop. Forever curious, as I want to understand things, learn about them. I have ruined more than a movie for my husband because I question what I see and I can predict what's going to happen, reveal the plot—yet another mute button I haven't found yet. I'm a nerd, I know. Or is there more to it?

Let's be honest. Who hasn't been window shopping on social media? Just scroll through the content, read it, and even have an opinion about it, or just like it without reacting? I certainly did in the beginning. I am an introverted, highly sensitive person, so engaging myself took me quite a while. Putting myself out there in the woods has been a challenge. And I believe I have overcome my fear of being the center of attention amongst the wolves. I, too, am a wolf now.

To be positive enhances positivity. It's a winning attitude. Seeing opportunities, possibilities, and potential will take us further. We see a future that's not there yet. But we know it will be.

Drops of Life Experience

💧

Whenever I see a negative hook, it stresses me, so I scroll out of there.

💧

Unfortunately, I see these features in today's kids, including mine. They are so spoiled by what our society offers them that they think no effort is needed. For instance, they look at YouTubers and imagine that having a good life is easy. No study, no school, just post silly videos about gaming online, and voilà, you're all set. I'm doing all I can to change their perspective, make it more realistic, and give them discipline. Teach them values. I hope I will achieve this goal or at least do damage control.

💧

Sure, nobody wants to waste their time. Besides health, time is our most valuable asset in life. Once it's gone, it's gone forever, so you must prioritize what you will spend it on.

💧

It works like reverse psychology, looking at things from another angle. I see the effect, too, on my husband when I ask for help in the household. If I say, "You have to do this . . ." he won't do it; however, if I say, "Could you help me with . . ." he (probably) will. Nobody likes being told what to do. If you make them feel they're doing something helpful, their reaction to the request differs.

I still see myself as a person, not a business. As an entrepreneur, I take all the actions and make the decisions. But a business? No.

I don't make myself get up early; my body has adapted itself naturally to the earlier sunrise. Our window is on the east side, so we wake up at dawn. And I enjoy the time I spend before the rest of them get up—the silence before the storm. I embrace that extra moment of peace.

I've been married for almost twelve years, and our open communication has been the glue holding us together. We always know what the other one is thinking; we discuss things openly, with no taboos. Even if it ends up in an argument, don't fear arguing. Expressing negative feelings, such as anger or frustration, is healthy, as long as you have mutual respect! No violence, physical or verbal! I always tell my kids that all violence is a sign of weakness. It means you can't express yourself using proper words, so you lash out at the other one to feel better about yourself. Be honest, be open, but always be respectful and constructive.

"Do. Or do not. There is no try." - Master Yoda.

Drops of life experience

Proud to be a nerd.

○

You never stop learning. To evolve is to live.

○

From the moment you decide your path, speed doesn't matter—motion matters. Please don't compare yourself to others. It's like comparing apples and oranges. We are all different, with different expectations and different voices. Follow your path.

○

I have never been a materialist, never believed in its value. The best things in life can't be bought.

○

To put my thoughts on standby (no mute button yet), I build with LEGOs or do a puzzle or a quiz. All those things keep my mind busy, so I can stop thinking about everything else. And even if I am still thinking, it's not the same, as this kind has a clear beginning and an end.

○

Find your place, and if you can't, make your own. That's what I did when the "regular" market was spitting me back out time after time. I went rogue (aka freelance) and created my own space in the world. We, as individuals, bring a uniqueness to the field, no comps, as there is only one you.

You cannot plan everything in life; you must trust that you'll know when the time comes. I'm forty-one and a mom of two, and I questioned my life so much when I was thirty-five. Some called it burnout; my therapist called it an existential crisis. Looking inside yourself and doing some critical soul-searching is all right. But don't forget to look at all you have done well in your life, all the presents. Be content; embrace what you have received. We are just human, after all. Plain and simple.

I strongly believe in the power of music. Just like art, the feeling music gives the listener depends on their inner needs. That's why everyone has their own taste in music. You hear it through your headset, just as you see through your glasses. A while ago, I posted about the power of music and how it helped me get through my father's eulogy. It will be three years on the 28th.

Credibility is my priority, and I'm focusing on it by showing my community who I am, my values, and what I'm all about. Once they appreciate me as a person, then they can see me as a potential coworker. First things first.

It makes no sense to consume information if you don't understand it. And it's not because you can read that you process the information and acquire its relevance. It would be best to let your brain cells work, and I'm not sure everyone uses them as they should. Take time to think about what you read, let it sink in, and think it through.

You don't just need to be capable of understanding the information you consumed (that's the technical part). Still, you also need to be willing to apply newly gained information (human factor). And politicians aren't renowned for changing their minds, even when they must confront an undeniable truth—for example, climate change. Their agenda (getting certain people what they want) is what most of them care about. But that's an entirely different discussion called "lack of integrity."

I learned a valuable lesson from psychology: "You already have a no, but you could get a yes." If you don't even ask or try, the answer is already no. However, if you ask, you might get a yes. It starts with the first step, your action toward your goal. Set yourself in motion; things can only change and go your way.

It's interesting to see how it is on the "other" side of writing. We all have the same goal: to deliver a good read.

If you think of writing as a form of art, one's expression should always be free of restrictions. Therefore, there are no wrong ways to do it. It's up to your reader to enjoy it or not. But the writer should write as it comes naturally to them. They must be truthful with themselves; that's what the reader expects.

💧

A mindset is a powerful tool, and we should use it more often.

💧

It can get quite stressful between fights and all kinds of existential drama.
Sometimes, I feel more like a referee than a mom.
When I see a significant offense, I will issue red cards and send them off the turf.

💧

One of the best features of art is its openness to interpretation. The artist started with a message in mind. However, depending on their search, the recipient will read into it unconsciously.

💧

Thanks to music and art, I found a way to speak up, even if that meant doing it in writing. I wrote my feelings on little Post-its and left them to be seen by the person I wanted to speak to. Today, I often still experience difficulties communicating freely in every circumstance; writing remains an efficient means to share my feelings. In the end, the most important thing is to communicate; it doesn't matter if you do it by voice, writing, or drawing . . . find your way, and as soon as you do, you'll feel the instant release, as you'll be free from those emotions.

Timing is essential in life, yet you can't plan for it. We meet too many unexpected variables. But, as you said, a result of bad timing doesn't define you. Therefore, follow your path, and you'll have new opportunities.

Resilience is a part of me; it helped me so many times in my life. I needed some courage to leap into being a solopreneur. You have to prioritize and think things through, especially with having kids and not being the youngest in the room anymore (not a grandma, either). Being a piano player helped me, as I learned to see what I needed to do next; I liked chess, too, as a child, but it has been a while. I'm a nerd, I know.

That's why I'm focusing first on building my credibility. That's the basis; once your community knows you are credible, trust will follow. Then I can offer my services. I'm not a salesman, and I hate being pushed into something. That's why I treat my community with the same respect I would like to receive. It's a two-way street.

That's what punching bags are for. Sometimes, you can't hold it in; as you said, dumping on others is not okay.

◊

Planning alone is not enough; there's no guarantee that you'll do it. Commit yourself to seeing things through. That's much more powerful than a note, as you made a promise to yourself.

◊

Some of the best things came from what we felt was a failure. It can be motivational therapy, "shock" therapy, or a wake-up call. A failure won't set us back; it's what we do next that defines our course.

◊

It's the best part of being a member of a community. Relationships matter: they can support, motivate, or sometimes even break you. So, it's essential to choose your relationships wisely.

◊

It's in our nature as moms to always prioritize, so it's no different when we think about how we spend our money. Even when you can afford it, you still balance value when buying something. I always ask myself, *Do we need this?* If the answer is no, I often don't believe it.

It's all easy when everything is going well. However, when facing dark times, you see who's really by your side to stay. We are all human. We all have our share of good and evil; however, many run from adversity. They bail. If you find the strength within yourself to pull through, the light on the other side will be the brightest you have ever seen.

◊

Finding the right people is the not-so-secret ingredient of a leader's success. Tools don't interact, don't engage, don't add a special something to your goal. People do.

◊

How wonderful it sounds to have had her grandmother as her mentor. Talk about a legacy. I wasn't quite so lucky, and I could only depend on myself at a very young age. But I try to be one for my kids. Teaching is so noble and valuable.

◊

I would add that after almost twelve years of marriage, we are free to be ourselves and accept each other. What a breath of fresh air when your partner is not trying to change you.

◊

Well, that s*cks. I understand the frustration, and I would be outraged. As they say, they might have won a battle but haven't won the war yet. Change your strategy and always be a step ahead of the ones who want to copy you.

◊

Perfection doesn't exist, and we should not strive to achieve it. It can only burn our spirit down.

◊

Change is what we tell in stories; otherwise, we wouldn't read them. It's the same thing in a movie; protagonists go through change, and that's what viewers want to see.

You should always try to look beyond the surface; otherwise, people like me (an introverted, highly sensitive person) will stay invisible forever. Not everyone can show their true selves simultaneously; some of us need more time to reveal ourselves, so take the time.

I'm a big fan of *Top Chef* (French edition), and one of the chefs always says, "Le mieux est l'enemi du bien," which means better is the enemy of the good. Why do you want to alter something that is good just as it is? There's no use; appreciate its simplicity.

Kindness is so underrated, and that's a pity, as it's such a simple and powerful tool. It can make a significant difference to one's life.

I think that's a trait of great leaders as well. You need to teach that life is not about getting what you want all the time; sometimes, no is just the best action at that time. It teaches you more than an easy yes, and when a no turns into a yes because you worked on it, your satisfaction will be even higher. I teach this to my kids as well.

💧

Wouldn't it be too obvious? I always see those kinds of hooks, and it's not original. I'm all about genuine communication, and I think I would be quite a hypocrite by following the mainstream to get more views. I don't think it would be meaningful to me. Just keep it real, even in the virtual world.

💧

I think it's a smart move, just like writing stuff on little notes. You never know when you could get inspired by it in the future. If you took the time to write it down, there must be a reason. If not? Just drop it!

💧

Humans are curious by nature. Otherwise, we wouldn't have researched and invented things. How can we entice our readers enough to keep reading without giving too much information?

💧

Parenting is so freaking hard that you must be prepared for any event 24/7. You can handle it, as long as it concerns you, but it's life-altering when it's about your child. My kids have a chronic illness that took years to diagnose. So, you do your best to be there, support them, and provide them with all they need. Day after day. Sending lots of positive vibes to you and your son.

◊

One of the best and most straightforward tips I read is that the second draft is the first draft minus 10 percent. That's an easy way to put it; anyone can apply it. As a writer, it's up to you to understand what can be deleted and written concisely. Just cut the cr*p in both ways.

◊

I instead focus on the positive things; we can constantly improve, of course, but I reverse that thinking:

1. Focus on the essentials.
2. Have a clear goal.
3. Keep questioning and stay curious.

It's just a mind trick, but as I always say, it is all about mindset. Change your perspective.

◊

Maybe it's because we expect more, especially from those closest to us. Society tells us to strive for excellence and impossible perfection, which influences our judgment, too.

◊

I learned far more from the school of life than from being taught. I'm always eager to learn; that's one of the things I love about LinkedIn. We learn from each other and share what we know in a simple manner.

◊

Always make time for yourself; it's not being selfish. If you don't take good care of yourself, you're not apt to care for others.

◊

They sell a state of mind, which makes you feel rich.

◊

Be grateful for the moments when everything is going right. Positive thoughts bring positive energy, which is spread around you.

◊

Why do we complicate our lives? Our grandparents knew it well. I know evolving is a part of our survival, yet we don't have to forget the simple things that are often the best.

◊

Words matter to bring clarity, as words do tell.

◊

Every time, I'm amazed by what the camera shows me. And maybe next time you walk down the street, you'll take the time to look up and down at the world surrounding you. Let yourself be amazed by it all.

◊

In this fast-paced world we live in, when time is on your side, it's like the universe is throwing you a bone. Be content with what is.

◊

While I was looking at a duck, swimming in the pond I kept thinking how wonderful his life must be. It looked
So peaceful,
So relaxed,
So simple.

Things must be bad if you're envious of a duck.

◊

Why do we tend to make things more complicated for ourselves?
Just keep it plain and simple.
It's all about mindset.
You've got the power within you to change things.

◊

Writing is a natural way of sharing your thoughts without expressing them directly.
It is such a blessing for an introverted, highly sensitive person

like me.
I'm grateful for this gift.

◊

It's not by denial that it didn't take place.
Neither by hiding its evidence that it won't reoccur.
We're disrespecting the author's work and taking the chance of making the same mistakes.
Let the past be.
It is our present and future that we need to worry about.

◊

Do you want to be healthy?
Do you want to be happy?
Do you want to succeed?
Do you want to evolve?
It's all about mindset.
Meaning, you can do it if you set your mind to it.

◊

With positive thoughts and simple faith, some things will work out just fine without any preparation. Confidence in what you're doing, to be correct. Life finds a way.

◊

By ignoring an act of injustice, we become an accomplice to it.

Drops of Life Experience

Be aware of what is happening around you, say no to violence of any kind, and raise your voice for those who can't. Justice starts with you.

◊

We can all read a recipe. However, we make it our own by adding the spices we love.
Some like extra salt.
Others like extra basil.
Few like extra pepper.
The same goes for writing, and we add what we love.

◊

As both function together in symbiosis,
there is no darkness if there is no light.
We accept them both as they come to us.

◊

Give it a try.
Every time you are stuck.
Every time you are in doubt.
Every time you are struggling.
Tell yourself,
Just keep it plain and simple.

◊

So, let the past be.
Find your peace with it.
Don't get blindsided by someone's attempt to keep your mind from what matters.
Understand the real issues and shift your focus to what you can do to bring significant change.
As it's our present and future, we need to worry about it.

◊

Laughter is an essential tool to relax our body and mind.
It makes us feel lighter and releases built-up tension.

◊

When you finally get to do what you love, it doesn't feel like work at all.
When you like what you do, you feel passion, which gives you energy.
I had to wait a long time to achieve this state of mind,
and even though I'm aware of being far from my financial goal, it still makes me happy.
I'm grateful for the opportunity and intend to make the best of it.

◊

I'm just a little woman, a mom of two, trying to create a fulfilling life for my kids.
But every small step can lead to great things.

Don't sell yourself short.
Believe in yourself, always.

I have an extraordinary power: I'm a fighter at heart.

◊

If you want things to change, take action and *be* the change.
If you long for things to improve, take action and *become* the best version of yourself.

◊

A disease impacts everyone, especially a rare illness, as you don't know what to expect.
The uncertainty brings a lot of stress and anxiety; however, knowing you are not facing this alone makes a significant difference.

◊

Thank you to all the caregivers.
Thank you to all those who are committed to helping people in need and their loved ones.
Thank you to science and research, always looking for answers and solutions.

◊

I am grateful for my husband and children. They are my motivation to go on every day.
I am thankful to my roommates for their unconditional

affection and companionship.

I am grateful for our home, keeping me and my family safe and sound.

○

When you're feeling under great pressure, about to break, remember some of the strongest and most
beautiful things in nature are built under pressure.

Hang on, keep going; your fight will end eventually; it won't last forever. No matter the outcome, at least you'll have given it your all; you won't regret it.

○

I was always told to treat others like I would want to be treated. However, how many of us apply this saying?

When was the last time you showed an interest in someone else?
Don't wait for others to take the first step, lead the way.

○

We often focus on what's not going our way and what we want to change. Even though it's easier to see what's wrong in your life, take a moment to focus on what's right. Focus on what you love or like.

Even in dark times, there is always something to be thankful for. Don't waste your time on what is missing; embrace the things you do have.

Drops of Life Experience

Being an '80s kid, I sometimes miss the days without the internet or smartphones.

Nowadays, we are constantly connected to the outside world, forcing us to process so much information at any given moment. As it becomes too much and makes me feel stressed and pressured, I allow myself to unplug and let my mind be offline for as long as it needs.

I'm pretty sure the outside world will also continue to go on.

People see things and understand them based on their knowledge and experience.

That's why someone's truth can be very different from someone who lived in the same situation. Not everything is what it seems at first sight. Take time to look closer before you decide you understand the problem.

It's a thin line before you become superficial.

We tend to take the highway that gets us from point A to Z as fast as possible. However, we risk missing out on many things; sometimes, the fastest way is not the best.

Get off the highway and take the small country roads. Take time to enjoy what's on your path.

If you stay on the highway, you will never see all the little things.

Relax and enjoy the ride.

Diversity makes the world a special place where different people meet to create something greater than themselves.
Diversity lays beauty and strength, as different minds can achieve more than those who think alike.

Be proud to be different, proud not to "fit in" with the crowd, as you are the secret ingredient that makes life's recipe unique.

Content, did you ever stop and reflect on the meaning of that word?
It means "satisfied or showing satisfaction with things as they are."
And that is powerful, and it changes your perspective on life and how you (re)act to it.
It's empowering as you learn to accept and appreciate rather than reject and demean.

Set yourself free from the burden of playing a part in life, which is the real deal.
Be courageous enough to show who you are through your emotions and own them before they become you.

Drops of Life Experience

You make time for the things that matter to you.
For time is the most beautiful gift you have to give.

Don't ever let people's negativity turn off your light.
Don't ever be afraid to shine on your own.
We are all unique, one of a kind.
Let your light shine brightly.

Even if you don't, I feel like it.
Even if you're afraid,
Just get up and start.
Just one step at a time.
Get up and start; you'll be closer to your goal than you were.

Kids today have easy and quick tools in their hands, making their curiosity and longing for research low.

We need to motivate them.
Let's do our part as parents.

I do embrace solitude.
Solitude is not the same as loneliness. Solitude is a choice you make for yourself to reduce the noise around you and listen to your inner self.

Labels aren't right for humans. We are more like puzzles; every puzzle piece makes us who we are, making us unique combinations.

You can't help everyone, or you can, but the results won't be as good. And if you're serious about your purpose of helping others, you want the results for the ones you help to be good.

Anticipatory anxiety, I get that too. Whenever I go somewhere, I'll go through the route I have to take in my mind. And if I need to make a pit stop at a store along the way, I need to know upfront so I can revise the route and my timing. I wouldn't say I like change or unexpected events of any kind. I need some time to adjust and rewire.

It's essential to remember at what level the person you're talking to is in their life when you give out advice. There is no "one fits all"; the advice needs to be tailored for them.

We all need more positive people in our lives.

My inner child returned to me after my accident and hasn't left me. I owe it to her to make our life the best I can.

◊

Have your priorities straight.
Health is a top priority, for without it, we ache.
Don't wait; take care of your body and listen to the signals. Your body is your greatest ally, yet it can become your worst enemy.

◊

You have to differentiate what kind of stress you're having, as there is positive stress that enhances your productivity and inspiration. However, negative stress causes physical and emotional distress. The latter is the one you should always avoid. It's essential to know the difference and act accordingly.

◊

My family is the essence of my life. It all starts and ends with them.

Conclusion

Life can be challenging and even feel extremely hard at times, but that doesn't mean it's impossible. And if I have found a way to cope, you can too. Why?

Because I am one of you, a trauma survivor and a chronic pain warrior, I have no particular or strong powers—just my strong will, which ensures I never give up.

Find your motivation, search for your path, and give it time to unfold.
And remember, you shouldn't go through this alone. You can find solace in a journal or talking to your partner or a good friend. And if that doesn't help, seek outside help.

Thanks to social media, you can follow me online, get inspired by my words, and even get in touch with me from your safe place at home. You'll find all my links on my website: www.pacha1.be

Don't be a stranger; let me know how you felt reading my book.
And if you enjoyed reading, you could relate to my words, and maybe you learned something new;
Please be so kind as to write a review. I would appreciate it, as I still need to grow and learn, too.
We are in this together.

Drops of Life Experience

Let your mindset be the driving force you need to self-improve to grow in life.

Don't forget to take care of yourself and make time for the things you love.

Make the most of it; that's all we can do in the end.

A collection of the author's best work thus far. She shares a personal tale about her hard knock life, divided into different drops; written in various styles: a memoir, storytelling, poetry, and quick thoughts. The author's purpose is to help and motivate other Trauma survivors and Chronic pain warriors by sharing her experience and lessons learned.
Chantal writes about life's joys and sorrows, wonders and aches. She shows how she managed to live a full life despite her struggles.

You **can** improve your quality of life too.

Mindset is your driving force
CHANTAL AGAPITI

www.ingramcontent.com/pod-product-compliance
Lightning Source LLC
LaVergne TN
LVHW020422070526
838199LV00003B/243